THE **EMDR** REVOLUTION

TAL
CROITORU

THE
EMDR
REVOLUTION
CHANGE YOUR LIFE
ONE MEMORY AT A TIME
The Client's Guide

NEW YORK

THE **EMDR** REVOLUTION
CHANGE YOUR LIFE ONE MEMORY AT A TIME

© 2014 **TAL CROITORU**. All rights reserved.

No part of this publication may be reproduced or transmitted in any form or by any means, mechanical or electronic, including photocopying and recording, or by any information storage and retrieval system, without permission in writing from author or publisher (except by a reviewer, who may quote brief passages and/or show brief video clips in a review).

Disclaimer: The Publisher and the Author make no representations or warranties with respect to the accuracy or completeness of the contents of this work and specifically disclaim all warranties, including without limitation warranties of fitness for a particular purpose. No warranty may be created or extended by sales or promotional materials. The advice and strategies contained herein may not be suitable for every situation. This work is sold with the understanding that the Publisher is not engaged in rendering legal, accounting, or other professional services. If professional assistance is required, the services of a competent professional person should be sought. Neither the Publisher nor the Author shall be liable for damages arising herefrom. The fact that an organization or website is referred to in this work as a citation and/or a potential source of further information does not mean that the Author or the Publisher endorses the information the organization or website may provide or recommendations it may make. Further, readers should be aware that internet websites listed in this work may have changed or disappeared between when this work was written and when it is read.

ISBN 978-1-61448-598-8 paperback
ISBN 978-1-61448-599-5 eBook
ISBN 978-1-61448-600-8 audio
Library of Congress Control Number: 2013944725

Morgan James Publishing
The Entrepreneurial Publisher
5 Penn Plaza, 23rd Floor,
New York City, New York 10001
(212) 655-5470 office • (516) 908-4496 fax
www.MorganJamesPublishing.com

Cover Design by:
Chris Treccani
www.3dogdesign.net

Interior Design by:
Bonnie Bushman
bonnie@caboodlegraphics.com

In an effort to support local communities, raise awareness and funds, Morgan James Publishing donates a percentage of all book sales for the life of each book to Habitat for Humanity Peninsula and Greater Williamsburg.

Get involved today, visit
www.MorganJamesBuilds.com.

TABLE OF CONTENTS

INTRODUCTION

- Have you been experiencing negative feelings for a significant amount of time, or are you experiencing negative feelings as the result of a crisis or traumatic event that don't seem to pass on their own?
- Do you feel that you have internal obstacles that prevent or inhibit you from advancing and breaking through, even though in theory you know what needs to be done?
- Have you noticed that you exhibit patterns of behavior that hinder you in your personal or professional life that awareness alone does not prevent you from repeating?
- Do you have unpleasant feelings, fears, or concerns that prevent you from speaking before an audience, cause you to feel uncomfortable being the center of attention, and block you from advancement in your personal or professional life?

The good news is that those conditions are reversible.

Even better news? Through a novel form of psychotherapy called Eye Movement Desensitization and Reprocessing (EMDR), the rate of change is faster than ever thought possible.

For example, did you know:

- EMDR is a psychotherapeutic treatment that yields meaningful results within weeks in cases where other methods take months or years to go into effect.
- Many studies confirm the effectiveness and success of the method within just a few therapy sessions.
- Millions of people have been successfully treated by this method.

Inside *The EMDR Revolution* you will discover the important information you need when feeling distressed or inhibited, as a way to select the appropriate help.

Reading the personal stories contained within will teach you a lot about yourself — what affects you, what motivates you, and what limits you. You deserve a better life. EMDR can help you heal your life, one memory at a time, and live the life you are meant to live.

"Since age 11 and my parents' traumatic divorce, I had been going to classic psychological therapy to help deal with both everyday life and difficulties from my earlier childhood. By age 26, I was worn out from years of therapy that really hadn't contributed much to my overall well-being, especially in relation to the amount of time, money, and effort I had invested. I could sit in a therapy session and talk about some childhood memory that I had discussed twenty times before, and I would still experience the same pain that I had always felt. I had cried countless times to my therapists, my friends, my family — and yet, none of the pain or trauma had diminished.

That's when I sought EMDR to give myself one last chance to receive the help that I so desperately needed. I was looking for something that would finally work and wouldn't take years to do the job. Even before I attended my first session, I made it clear that I was looking for something that could help me in a short period of time: I had already spent 15 years in therapy and was not looking to invest a lot more time.

I got more out of EMDR than I could have ever imagined. The work was intense, but almost immediately I felt the effects of it. This made me actually start to look forward to the intense sessions: I knew that it would hurt, but then the pain would be gone and I would be healed.

For the first time in my life, I truly felt that therapy was effective and I have finally overcome the trauma that accompanied me for most of my life. When I choose to, I can talk about my childhood — but now, I do not re-live the pain that accompanied it. I have also become much more connected to myself and my family members since I have been able to let go of the hurt and fear that had prevented me from doing so in the past".

OR "HOW IN GOD'S NAME DID I NOT HEAR OF THIS BEFORE?"

Before hearing of EMDR, I was a clinical social worker, working in a private practice, treating clients who came to me due to a crisis or emotional distress. I believed I was doing a pretty good job — my clients were relatively happy, experienced changes, and recommended me to others. What more could I ask for?

And then, a young woman in a very serious state came to see me after a traumatic event. She was extremely overwhelmed and suffering so much, that I suggested she consider going to a psychiatrist in order to get anti-depressants and anti-anxiety drugs. I treated clients in this condition before, but it was always accompanied by pharmaceutical treatment. However, due to the client's religious beliefs, she was afraid the psychiatric treatment would hurt her chances of a potential future match for an arranged marriage. She refused outright.

I was consulting a more experienced therapist who told me that if this was the case, I should just be with her in her pain. I did not accept this advice. If it were me on the other side, I wouldn't want someone that would just be with me in my pain, in the same manner that if I had aches in my back I wouldn't want the M.D. to just be with me in my pain. I think that as therapists we should fight for more.

During my quest for new ideas, I stumbled upon a book at the bookstore called, *The Instinct to Heal: Curing Depression, Anxiety and Stress without Drugs and Talk Therapy*, written by French psychiatrist, Dr. David Servan-Schreiber. I was immediately attracted to the title because I had never really connected professionally to the "Freudian" therapy method, and "without drugs" was exactly what the client wanted; I hurriedly rushed to buy and read it. Two chapters in the book were about a therapeutic method called EMDR or Eye Movement Desensitization and Reprocessing. It was a method I had never heard of; not in university and not at any phase of my mental health training in the psychiatric ward or mental health clinic. The things written there were so amazing to me that it literally caused my jaw to drop.

In the book, Dr. Servan-Schreiber wrote of his own skepticism when first hearing of EMDR, and talked about the studies he read that melted his skepticism away. One study, published in one of the most rigorous journals in clinical psychology focused on 80 patients with serious mental trauma who were treated with EMDR over three 90 minute sessions. This group of patients experienced an 80% success rate of patients who no longer felt symptoms of post-traumatic stress (PTSD).

Just three sessions. Three!

How in the world did this take place in three sessions and not three years' worth of sessions? According to what I had been taught, and what I witnessed at the mental health clinic where I was trained in the past, PTSD was considered a chronic, ongoing condition. People with PTSD were in treatment for 6, 7 and even 10 years without much of a change; how could three sessions change what 10 years could not?!

Moreover, Dr. Servan-Schreiber stated, when the research subjects were interviewed 15 months later to see if the results had lasted, it was found that not only had they lasted, but the patients had even improved. He wrote that in spite of his psychoanalytic background, the results he read about convinced him to learn how to treat with EMDR. After using the method, he concluded that he could no longer ignore what, time and time again, he saw in his clients.

Likewise, I felt I had to find out more — more about what it was and how it could work — because based on what I previously learned, it sounded too good to be true. The dawning notion came to my mind — perhaps the problem laid in what I had been taught and not in what I had just discovered. I rushed to get more information, and attended a lecture by Israeli psychologist who had participated in a humanitarian mission to treat Congolese women. These women had been raped by soldiers from rival tribes. With their bodies ravaged and mutilated, their families and tribes shunned them.

The mission lasted for a few weeks and the psychologist returned with databases and videos of these women, documenting them before and after EMDR treatment.

I left the lecture mumbling to myself, "Dear God, if it so quickly helps Congolese women who are in such a severe state, I have to learn this as well; my clients are in much better shape, so it surely can help them even faster".

I started studying EMDR and learning more and more. In the years since, I have made EMDR my life's work. I was exposed to an enormous amount of research that proved the effectiveness of treating with EMDR. The more I used EMDR, the more I saw proof of its positive effects — first in my own clinic and later on in my national chain of clinics.

I saw more and more people. In the beginning I was a "refuge" for people who had given up on standard psychotherapy because it hadn't, or had barely, helped them at all, even after three, six or even seven years. For the majority using EMDR, their condition improved within a few sessions, and the treatment ended to their satisfaction within weeks to a few months.

As I thought, what worked extremely quickly for life-threatening traumatic events turned out to work just as quickly for events that were not as severe.

I also saw a study that found that non-life threatening events, such as divorce and unemployment, for example, could still generate post traumatic symptoms; equally or even more than life-threatening events. Just like my colleagues in the U.S. and Europe, who have been utilizing EMDR for more than 20 years, I started offering EMDR therapy for a broader array of anxieties and obstacles than just PTSD. For example: life crises (divorce, cheating, dismissal from employment), improved functioning at work, exam anxiety, and even improved athletic performance or improved performance for musicians. Chapter 2 details how EMDR works. In it you will see what a musician with stage fright and a man who caught his wife cheating on him have in common, and how both can be helped in the same way.

Some of my clients remained in therapy after the initial problem that brought them to therapy was resolved, in order to work on other aspects of life. In each case, just a few short weeks were enough to treat another inhibition. In some, we managed to treat them in such a way that their lives turned around completely; beginning with the initial crisis that was resolved in the best way possible, through dramatically improving the occupational aspect of life; and, finally, the broader personal, and even sporting and performing abilities. Later, while working with the Israeli Ministry of Foreign Affairs, diplomatic staff and families who had experienced a traumatic event were referred to me and brought to Israel. Those diplomatic clients usually left two to three weeks later without PTSD symptoms. How does the saying go? "There's nothing like it!"

Time and time again, when talking to colleagues, mainly overseas and also in Israel, I heard about similar dynamics for considerable and fast improvement. Some of them received financing for only 10 sessions from the insurance companies, some for only four, and still, such dramatic improvements were seen that even several years of treatment via other methods had not necessarily brought about such progress.

The most common question I get is, "How come I've never heard of this before?" and it breaks my heart. Like the client of mine who said it after 15 years of therapy with a string of other therapists in treatment methods that didn't help enough. Another client is a therapist herself, and wondered what she had been doing with her own clients all these years when she herself was helped within 4 sessions. There are also people who dragged their misery around with them for years; who didn't pursue treatment because they didn't want to pay that kind of money and spend that much time, and didn't understand how a stranger who would only listen to them for less than an hour a week could improve their situation (and very rightfully so in my opinion. See Chapter 6, which deals with my own philosophy about therapy).

Most people haven't heard of EMDR because the method was developed in the late 1980's (1987, to be exact), and it usually takes many years for a psychological treatment method to become common knowledge.

In the U.S. EMDR was used after the Oklahoma City bombing, the Columbine massacre, and 9/11. This method has been used to treat victims of natural disasters in the West and in the Far East (hurricanes and tsunamis). In addition, EMDR has been used more and more in a wide range of fields, such as drug problems. As early as the 1990's, there were reports about the success of EMDR in treating exam anxiety and in improving sports achievements.

In the public sector like hospitals and public mental health clinics, the use of EMDR still focuses on the initial therapeutic goal it was developed for: post-traumatic stress.

Over the years, as the rate at which people approached me increased, I finally came to the conclusion that now was the right time to achieve a wider vision — to make a contribution to change the way psychotherapy is done in my country — and beyond, and to inform the public at large about EMDR, that was found many years ago effective in assisting a wide range of suffering and crises, from hindering behavior patterns on one hand, to eradicating internal obstacles and improving achievements on the other.

In 2011 I took the first step towards greater influence — I established a national chain of EMDR clinics in my country.

This book is the second step in my vision — to bring valuable information about EMDR to the general public and break common myths about psychotherapy.

This book includes case studies and examples. Some details were altered in order to maintain the privacy and confidentiality of the clients. However, other details, including the length of time the clients were in process, are true.

If you have any comments at all about the book, please feel free to contact the author: tal@emdrexperts.com

"*I was going through a very rough patch in my personal life. I was a new mother, but instead of being happy and enjoying the baby, as I had always imagined I would, I would get irritated with him all the time. I was angry, screaming and impatient. I would cry all the time and daily situations appeared as insurmountable obstacles. I felt unable to deal with any challenge. I didn't even have energy to deal with my husband, and would get impatient with him. I would argue and angrily explode at him in tears at regular intervals. This was coupled with unbearable feelings of guilt, especially regarding my son who was saddled with such an evil mother. The only place where I could maintain a semblance of sanity was at work, but it took a lot of energy and I felt drained.*

In the first session with Tal I just told her my story. I emerged tired and exhausted, and asked myself why I even need this. In the second session we got to work. I already achieved very important insights. After the session, I kept testing myself: do I really believe in these insights? Is the change real, from within? The answers were always yes.

I began noticing its influence at home — my patience slowly improved, I was able to enjoy my son and felt much more competent.

In the third session we continued working, I got to work on several memories and incidents in a single session, and afterwards simply felt like I had returned to the real me.

First of all, the guilt simply disappeared. I felt as if 20 lbs. of hardships had fallen by the wayside. I felt more alive and able to once again enjoy the simple things in life, from my son's smile to my husband's embrace. Even my husband noticed a change and felt like he finally got his wife back. Mainly, I felt complete with myself and who I was, with the kind of mother and spouse I was, and with everything I did.

After the third session, Tal and I had to stop because of the holidays, but I already knew I reached my goal, and knew I would simply be returning for the 4th session to thank Tal for changing my life and for making me myself again.

It's hard to describe in words how such a profound change can come about via so few therapy sessions. It sounds unreal, but lo and behold, it's here. I recommend EMDR treatment to anyone who experiences difficulties. As a therapist myself, I cannot wait to learn the method myself and spread the word".

CHAPTER 1

WHAT IS EMDR, AND HOW DOES IT DIFFER FROM THE PSYCHOLOGICAL TREATMENT METHODS THAT PREDATE IT?

E MDR stands for Eye Movement Desensitization and Reprocessing:

Desensitizing the intensity of the emotion felt while recalling the traumatic event.

Reprocessing the memories of the traumatic events that did not undergo the needed processing in real time.

Eye movements were originally used to make sure that the two hemispheres of the brain took an active part in the processing procedure (see chapter 2 for how EMDR works). Today, additional methods are used, such as earphones playing sounds intermittently to both sides of the brain, or palm vibrations firing off intermittently.

The method was developed by Dr. Francine Shapiro, a psychologist, in 1987.

As mentioned, the method was originally used to treat post-traumatic events for American servicemen dealing with traumatic memories after the Vietnam War. Later on, the method was used in other traumatic circumstances as well. Since the treatment of traumatic events is funded mainly by governments and insurance companies who require definitive proof of its effectiveness, EMDR is among the most thoroughly researched psychological methods, and many studies attest to its effectiveness within just a few therapeutic sessions. **Only after EMDR had time and time again shown its effectiveness in difficult cases it was then used with less difficult situations.**

Remember, EMDR is a psychological method in every respect. This means that only therapists trained in mental health therapy (mostly requiring a Master's degree as a minimum), and who have been specifically trained in how to administer EMDR, are licensed to treat using this method. EMDR is recognized by leading associations such as the American Psychological Association and the American Psychiatric Association.

And yet, it is different from all psychological methods that pre-date it.

First, compared to previous methods it is usually found more effective (better results, or equivalent results in a shorter time period). Such differences in duration of treatment and degrees of effectiveness are unprecedented in the history of psychotherapy.

Second, defining the problem and the possibility of treating it, and the focus of the therapy, are different from all other forms of psychotherapy. In EMDR, the negative beliefs, the emotional suffering, and the "non-advancing internal story" (what is called paradigms in the personal development field) are not the problem. Those are the symptoms of an experience, or previous life experiences, that our brains did not manage to process in real-time. Those unprocessed memories are the problem.

At certain times in our lives, events took place that overwhelmed us, whether because we were not at our best at the time, or because of the severity of the event; our brain was "flooded" and could not properly process the event when it happened. The result was that the impressions of the event — thoughts, feelings, body sensations, pictures and smells — were kept unprocessed, in raw form, by the brain.

When a present event connects to such a traumatic event from the past, it serves as a trigger for the activation of the unprocessed contents. These contents, which were kept in their raw state — thoughts, feelings, emotions — rise up again in their raw state. In such a situation, we feel in the present as we did while the past event was happening.

With EMDR, we locate the traumatic memories that are responsible for our present-day distress (in EMDR understanding those connections can be done very quickly, and it usually takes 1-3 sessions), and then we begin to reprocess them.

Once the event has been reprocessed, new events in the present will not serve as triggers for the same feelings that were experienced in the past. The reactions in the present stop being the result of the unprocessed events from the past. In accordance with the basic assumptions of the therapy, once the reprocessing has finished, the symptoms of the negative beliefs, or negative internal emotions that lead to the negative feelings, will disappear. The treatment with EMDR includes an abundance of insights and "falling chips", but unlike most other methods, the client achieves these insights **on his own** because of the process, and just as importantly, he does so in a very short time.

In EMDR, we do not provide tools to deal with the problem, but rather remove the problem. When the problem is removed, the symptoms cease to exist. You can think about it like this:

A man was walking along a riverbank. As he was walking, he noticed people in the water who were drowning, so he began to reach in to save them. He kept saving until one day he got up and left. When he was asked, "Where are you going? Who will save all these drowning people?"

the man replied, "I am going to see who is throwing them off the bridge".

There are therapy methods in which the basic principle is to create an awareness of responses, and the triggers that set them off. Slowly but surely clients are helped to become aware of the fact that, not only are there "people in the water" (i.e., there is a problem that must be solved), but there is also "someone who is throwing them into the water" (past events).

Different therapy methods focus on changing the response. With these methods, clients learn how to "better help the people in the water" (representing distress or inhibitions at present), to more quickly realize that someone is about to drown. Therefore those methods try to improve swimming techniques, to quickly get that person out of the water so that the time in the water is not too long — meaning, that the clients are provided with tools to deal with the times that they feel distressed. For example, a client suffering from exam anxiety will practice relaxation techniques when he becomes anxious, or techniques to fight off the anxiety-causing thoughts.

In contrast, the EMDR approach works on changing the stimulus — so that the circumstance will no longer provoke negative emotions to begin with. We do not provide the tools, but rather remove the 'hooligan' who threw the people off the bridge (while working via a focused, fast, efficient method to neutralize the effect of past events, so symptoms are not activated in the present).

A demonstration of the differences between treatment methods on a common type of performance anxiety, such as exam anxiety:

Exam anxiety, in its narrowest sense, is an anxiety that appears in students when tested, either orally or in writing, by someone at an educational institution. In its wider sense, a person could experience such anxiety at job interviews, evaluation centers, presentations in front of an audience, and even during sex. Therefore, those who survived the time in school and thought they had left such anxieties behind them, often find out that this is not the case.

In traditional therapy, the therapist, alongside the client, tries to find the source of the anxiety. Focus is put on the past; they are helped to understand how their parents pressured them, and how their self-esteem was based on "delivering the goods". In this way, ultimately, the client becomes aware of the sources of his anxiety. Unfortunately, mere awareness does not help it disappear.

In the biofeedback method, clients are helped to acquire tools to monitor the anxiety, so that when they feel it is coming near, they can relax it; using such methods as breathing, etc.

In Cognitive-Behavioral Therapy (CBT), clients are taught to argue with the "distorted thoughts", such as the thought that they must "deliver the goods", and to find an alternative way of thinking every time the anxiety strikes. The premise is that in this way the anxiety will fade. At the same time, clients are exposed to exam-like situations in order to practice.

In EMDR therapy, clients locate the key events that caused these sensations and made the connection between an exam state and the anxiety and then reprocess them. After processing the key events related to the source of the anxiety, the person will not feel anxious about exam situations in the future. This means that the client will not acquire tools to deal with the anxiety that is brought on by the exam state, like those in the previous two methods discussed, and will not get homework like in CBT, but will rather undergo a quick and focused process that will lead to the exam no longer provoking anxiety.

The unique aspects of EMDR can be summarized in a sentence I heard from a client in her late 20's who had been in other forms of therapy prior to starting EMDR for almost 15 years (!) without achieving real progress. For her, what could not be attained in 15 years using the traditional methods, such as Psychodynamic and Cognitive therapies, could be attained with EMDR in just a few months. Towards the end of our sessions together, she told me, "In the past, when the therapist told me that something that happens to me is because of my past, it would cause me to get even more depressed. What can I possibly do about my past? It's not like I have a time machine. Today, every time I find out that something that bothers me is because of my past, I am really glad, since I know that I can bring it up at the next EMDR session, and it will not bother me anymore".

For whom is the treatment appropriate?

As mentioned, originally, the method was developed for treating post-traumatic stress. The first clients were veterans of the Vietnam War, as well as sexual assault victims. The findings were quite different from findings of previous treatment methods; people who had suffered for years and decades, some taking part in therapies which were of no help, recovered from the post-trauma symptoms within a few sessions. Before that, post-trauma was considered a chronic and ongoing disorder.

After having been found effective time and time again EMDR was expanded in three different directions:

First, for **people whose condition was less severe than that of post-trauma**. For example, people suffering from anxiety, depression, phobias, life crises such as divorce, difficulties in establishing intimate relations, low self-esteem, etc.

Second, for **people who wished to improve achievements in various areas**. EMDR was found to be effective in improving academic achievements, including treating exam anxiety, working with athletes before competitions or during recovery from injury, working with performers such as musicians and actors, businessmen, dealing with business crises and removing internal inhibitions from business and personal growth.

Third, for **people with severe mental and emotional disorders**, such as those suffering from addictions, severe psychiatric disorders such as bi-polar disorder and schizophrenia, dissociative disorders, and even people with mental retardation who underwent trauma. In such cases, EMDR could be incorporated, preferably with more extensive therapy. This book will focus on the first two groups.

For what ages is EMDR appropriate?

EMDR can be used to treat children in whom treatment was found to be faster when compared to adults. At very young ages, the treatment is done in the presence of the parents.

No one is too old for EMDR therapy, as long as the individual has the ability to cope. I have personal experience treating clients in their 70's, and have heard from colleagues overseas, and in Israel, about the success of EMDR therapy for people in their 80's and 90's.

Summary: In which kinds of situations is EMDR useful?

Eliminating internal obstacles to achieve your personal best such as: Athletes looking to boost their performance results before a big race; students before exams, SAT's, etc.; artists before performances and auditions; business people looking to improve their ability to mount successful presentations and negotiations, and improve their self-worth before a request for a raise or promotion.

Dealing with life crises such as: Betrayal, divorce, unemployment, birth trauma, etc.

Changing repetitive behavioral patterns such as: Difficulty forming intimate relationships, recurring bad decision making, tantrums, etc.

Dealing with anxiety and phobias such as: Fear of public speaking, performance anxiety, driving anxiety, fear of dogs, dental phobia, recurrent nightmares, etc.

Dealing with traumatic events such as: Sexual assault, physical assault, car accidents, terror attacks, death of a loved one, etc.

Suffering or inhibitions can be the result of medical or biochemical conditions and/or the result of life experiences that have been experienced in the past or being experienced today. **When it comes to mental suffering or internal inhibition caused by life experiences, EMDR can be helpful**.

How is it that EMDR can be used to treat so many types of problems?

Despite, of course, the differences in the details, the neuropsychogenic mechanisms causing the distress in the present because of events in the past, are mostly the same. In EMDR it is not the role of the therapist to scratch his beard or give commentary, or give advice based on personal experience. His job is to help complete the processing of the events that are at the heart of the present inhibition or distress. The details come from the client, not the therapist. I will explain more about this in the next chapter.

"I am 40 years old, married with 4 children. I live in a small village with my family. I work and happily raise the children, surrounded by family and friends; trying to catch up with time. Two years ago I gave birth to my youngest son, a fourth pregnancy that started with the calmness of a mother who had been through three pregnancies and thought she knew everything.

In the 24th week, in the middle of a family vacation, I started feeling pressure from labor pains and was put on a very long bed rest... weeks of lying in bed worrying about the little baby inside me. I made daily calculations and was incessantly worried about his weight, his chance of survival, birth defects and other endless concerns and anxieties.

On the first day of the 36th week, a healthy 2.7 Kg baby was born in a short, exhilarating delivery. For the first time in months I breathed a sigh of relief and held my baby. There were so many moments when I feared I would never see that day. But... my happiness was premature and short-lived. Two hours after the birth, when I was in my room, happy that the nightmare was behind me, my medical condition started deteriorating. I seemed to be on a rollercoaster, quickly falling into a deep, dark abyss.

Ten days of intensive care followed, I hovered between life and death. Looking into my husband's eyes, I worried he might have to raise 4 orphans alone. Trying not to let fear overtake me, I fought for every breath, between consciousness and fog, fighting to choose life with all my might. I begged to hold the baby I fought so hard to give life to, and who I now needed to touch, to give me the strength to struggle, not give up, and stay alive. I looked the intensive care doctor in the eye and saw helplessness, her eyes said, 'We already tried everything, and desperation is taking over.' Realizing this must be the end, I sunk into a black hole… the doctor, divine powers, my will to live or all combined, and the minute all hope was lost I returned to life.

After a few more days of recovery in the hospital, I begged to come home to the family I wanted so badly to be so close to.

Tired, physically weak, but a tiger mom, I resumed full functioning immediately. I breastfed, cooked and managed my household — the kingdom of parents and 4 children. I didn't stop to think, feel or talk about what had happened. I was 'mother earth,' with a smiling mask, running forward. Everything that happened in intensive care was stored in a sealed box and placed deep within the back of my mind.

Two years went by, and on the face of it everything returned to normal. I quickly went back to work, the children grew up, and the super sweet baby was already running around.

And one clear day, I was in a terrorist attack. A sudden fear of death (literally) took me over and didn't let go. Body shaking, overcome with tears, feeling helpless, the body loosening, unable to cope, I just cried, cried, cried. I, invincible me, could not understand what was happening.

I was not hurt, but I was surrounded by a strong sensation of death and nights full of nightmares. Waking up in the middle of the night feeling suffocated, I felt like I was going to die. I could not function. I wanted the kids to be taken away, and be on my own.

After a few days, a friend who came to visit held me tight, looked me in the eye and said, 'Honey, you're suffering post-traumatic stress from the birth.' The bombing was merely a catalyst that made the birth trauma break out.

My dear friend linked me to Tal Croitoru, an EMDR therapist specializing in post-traumatic stress. I didn't know the method, and I didn't think this was PTSD or that I warranted therapy. I felt my reaction was natural for the situation I was in, as if I had taken 2 steps forward; I could have gotten seriously hurt.

But a session was scheduled, and I felt bad about cancelling it (we also found time to treat these feelings). In the first session I spat out the whole story like a machine gun. Step by step. What I went through during bed rest, fears and worries about the baby, the birth and the complications that followed. I spoke in torrents (a story no one had ever heard in full until then), and Tal sat and listened. At the end of the first session I told Tal I was going to go abroad for a while, and had only two weeks to devote to therapy. Tal could not see what the problem was. She told me that with EMDR you can treat and solve post-traumatic stress very quickly. What were required were very frequent sessions (almost every day, for 2 hours at a time) I was very skeptical — who can fix PTSD in two weeks?!

We met the next day; me, Tal and my skepticism.

Tal let me hold the pulsers and I began telling her about the pregnancy and birth from the start. I could not control my thoughts as they were gushing out. At first, I really struggled with them. I wanted them to go where I thought was right, but the body is wise and the thoughts know where they should go. Tal saw my discomfort and laughed: "Even if you're thinking that you want an avocado sandwich, just go with that…" so the thoughts continued to flow until all of a sudden, they screeched to a halt due to a difficult situation (which I didn't even remember). Tal asked questions (about its difficulty) and again, I thought about it. Tal tried to quantify how much it upset me, and to my surprise the traumatic situation that had earlier been untouchable, suddenly disturbed me less. Again, Tal didn't let go, and began instructing me. I began reliving the moment with the two pulsers in my hand and a racing uncontrollable mind… Suddenly, minute by minute, I felt the hardship and pain melting like a block of ice. We moved on to treat another difficult moment and again with Tal's questions my mind raced between being unable to touch it, to feeling like this was something I could contain. After 4-5 sessions I felt like the severe trauma was behind me. I was now free to work on my behavior patterns and things that were hard for me. The serious feelings of death, inability to breathe and specific moments over the previous two years that I had been unable to deal with or remember, were now tolerable.

I found myself sitting with my mother and sister and for the first time, without crying, telling them in detail what had happened. I felt these things, but I could now contain them.

In therapy, I realized how unaware I was of the anger I had towards the baby I had wanted so much. I realized suddenly, that I subconsciously felt like I might have died because of his birth, and leave my precious family without a mother. I didn't remember if I held my son after the birth and it tore me apart. Tal took me back to that magical moment and I was suddenly there. I could clearly see my baby coming into the world and the doctor giving him to me. The feeling of happiness flooded over me and allowed me to experience the attachment to my baby that I had missed because of the turn of events.

Ten days of intensive treatment almost every day; a shocking, exhausting treatment in which little was said. I was mostly with myself, holding the pulsers, with my mind playing through the events. I literally saw moment upon moment, and things I hadn't remembered popped up. I experienced fast, uncontrollable thoughts, and a powerful return to the situation, so much so that I could see, feel and smell it. A second after, Tal, without knowing what is going through my mind, told me to stop where it is hard and asked me to gauge its difficulty on a scale of 0-10. She then took me back to the situation until it faded.

It seems unreal, but after only three sessions, the feeling of relief was enormous. I suddenly felt physically light. I realized the block of anxiety was stuck in my soul and didn't let me enjoy things to their full extent, especially my beautiful child.

I finished the therapy and happily went on the trip I had planned, holding my dear child and incredibly grateful to my friend who insisted I get help.

I have no doubt I would have spent years in regular therapy, week after week, retelling the fears and anxieties without a solution. Here, in less than two weeks, the trauma went from a monster I could not wake up to a difficult experience I could contain, and one that didn't take over my life or interfere with daily functioning. I no longer see images at night of myself leaving this life, and I no longer wake up in the middle of the night feeling like I cannot breathe. I can now talk about the experience I went through without weeping. Most importantly, I'm not the least bit angry at my baby, and I'm glad I got pregnant and gave birth to him. My beloved family has a mother who regained herself thanks to the swift treatment".

CHAPTER 2

HOW DOES EMDR WORK?

Why would something that happened in the past, even in the distant past, keeps bothering us?

We have various physiological mechanisms, in our bodies, whose job is to lead us on the path to health and recovery. If there is a cut or fracture in the body, the body works to heal it. In a similar fashion, when we undergo emotional turmoil, our brain tries to work to process the experience — during waking and sleeping hours.

When certain events occur that are overwhelming for us — because the event is so powerful, or because we were too weak (due to lack of sleep, disease), or because we were helpless (as we are when we are young) — our brain cannot complete processing the event in real-time.

This results in the incident being stored in our memory in an unprocessed fashion — raw — with the sights, smells, voices, feelings, thoughts, and body sensations from the time that it happened. Memories stored in this raw fashion are kept separate from the general memory network, in a kind of separate "capsule", which does not have access to earlier or later memories.

Therefore, unless an external intervention will take place, no matter what happened or will happen later on, the content of the "capsule" that contains the memory in its raw form will not change. Every time there is an external stimulus in the present that touches the content in the capsule, the content may "replay" — in its raw form — and we feel feelings from the past in the present, with an intensity unsuited to present-day events.

The classic example is that of shell shock: When a door is slammed, it might sound like gunshots. The man with shell shock might feel that he is on the battlefield again, along with the sights, feelings, and thoughts related to those past events. It happens, despite the fact that the person knows cognitively, and beyond a doubt, that the war is over and years have passed since that event, etc.

Most people do not suffer from PTSD, yet they definitely have traumatic memories that play out in later situations in a way that does not advance them, but hurts them. We see situations such as: An adult who is extremely fearful due to a small dog (because the content of the capsule — a dog biting him at the age of 4 was playing out), a senior official losing his authority over lesser officials (because the content of the capsule — contained a period in his life when he was weaker), wealthy people who still feel poor (due to capsule content from an earlier period), fear of driving (the car accident stored in the capsule), fear of flying (capsule of the flight that contained turmoil), fear of public speaking (capsule of that mishap in elementary school), unpleasantness when passing in front of a particular café (capsule with the memories of the "ex" with whom we often sat there), avoiding asking for a raise/promotion (capsules of previous events of feeling "not good enough"), lack of confidence in social connections (capsule of being excluded in elementary school), or lack of self-confidence in intimate relations (capsule of those who hurt me when I trusted them), etc.

In other words, every time an incident overwhelms us in such a way that the brain cannot process the incident in real-time, while it is happening, or very close to it, a capsule is formed with a piece of us stuck in the incident, so that we are actually reliving the incident over and over again. It has nothing to do with logic, since the logic is in the adaptive memory network to which the traumatic memory has no access. We can tell ourselves over and over that the event is in the past, is no longer part of our lives, in fact it hasn't been for years, and shouldn't affect us anymore, yet it is not accessible to the content of the capsule, because it is stored in a separate network. This is how, for example, people who go to therapy for years can spend endless sessions crying over the same key hurtful incidents over and over again (since what is playing in the capsule is painful), etc.

A good example of what we are talking about, one which I came across in the therapy room, is Nina, whose son was born prematurely several years ago. When she went to see her son in the neonatology unit, she was horrified to see the physicians performing CPR on him. Despite many attempts, she was not allowed to go near him and was sent away, claiming that her presence would only hinder the CPR attempts. She spent the next few hours alone outside the department, in intense fear and anxiety. As far as she was concerned, her son was dying or was on the brink of death, and she reacted accordingly. Those were the memories of the incident locked away in a separate capsule in her memory.

Two hours later, she was allowed to enter the unit to find that a mix-up had occurred. The baby who underwent CPR was in fact, not her son. Her son was in good health and was released from the hospital several hours later. His development was fine as well.

In accordance with such a troubling experience, the traumatic experience of those two hours outside the neonatology unit was stored in a "capsule" which was separated from Nina's general memory network. Therefore, the incident of her son's life being in danger remained a vivid memory, despite being an absolute mistake, only realized afterwards. When we began working with the memory. Nina categorized the degree of disturbance in the present of this past memory as a 10, the highest degree. This scale of 0-10 in therapy, is called Subjective Units of Disturbance (SUD), and is also used at a later stage to measure improvement. Even though it had not actually been her son, the memory disturbed her to the highest degree. Even before the end of the first hour of therapy, after having incorporated content from her general memory network into the raw event capsule, Nina categorized the disturbance as 0, meaning that the memory no longer triggered negative feelings at all.

Different capsules with similar characteristics may group to form a common theme, made up of thoughts such as "I am not good enough" or "I must be disturbing". Dealing with such a theme during therapy is like trying to get rid of a big block of ice. You do not try to melt it all at once, rather, you cut a piece of it and melt it, and then another, and one by one, the 'ice chips' melt away. That is the reason this book's subtitle is *Change Your Life One Memory at a Time*. Systematic work minimizes the influence of the theme and can even make it disappear completely.

In EMDR therapy, the history is collected in usually 1-3 sessions, with an emphasis on the history of "capsules" relevant to what is bothering the client — distress/inhibition/partial living up to your potential at present. Afterwards, we make sure that the client has enough resources to process it, and, if so, immediately begin to work. If not, we first equip him with enough resources, and only then begin to systematically complete the processing of the raw data found in those "capsules" that are separated from the general memory network.

Each capsule is reached by four different channels: the **sensory channel** (mostly visual, but sometimes smell and/or sound), the **emotional channel**, the **cognitive channel** (which negative beliefs are associated with the memory, and which positive beliefs the client would like to be associated with the memory once the processing is done. In appendix G you can find a list of both common negative beliefs, and common positive beliefs.), as well as the channel of **physical/body sensations**.

The raw, traumatic content includes, in many cases, the bodily sensations from the time of the event. Therefore, while working with an injury, actual physical pain might recur in the affected body part, but will disappear shortly after the processing has been completed. For example, while working with a client on self-inflicted wounds, pains in the scars from the old wounds appeared; while working with a man injured in the army, the pain of the injury was felt once more.

It is common for a client to experience pain in an afflicted body part, even years after the injury, due to the bodily sensations channel. An example of this is "phantom limb pain", which appears in patients who, despite having lost a limb, still feel the pain. For example, an amputee might feel strong pain in his leg, despite the fact that he does not have one anymore. This phenomenon is treated as a purely medical one. However, in recent years, several researchers have shown success in treating such pain with EMDR. With the processing of the traumatic memory, the physical pain connected to this memory that kept on being "replayed" as long as it was stored in a separate area in the brain as a traumatic memory, disappeared.

More than once, people make the mistake of thinking that memories that are relevant to therapy are events that haunt them in a conscious and daily manner, such as recurrent nightmares of a specific incident. However, relevant events do not have to be so. That is, these are incidents that the client might remember, but might not be aware of their effect on him. For example, a client says, "Yes, she pushed me and called me a dirty Jew, but I was eight years old then, now I'm 40 and live in Israel. I do not think it still bothers me". But as mentioned before, the traumatic memory is stored in a separate capsule and does not function according to the laws of our known logic. Therefore, the way to quantify the impact on the client at present is not by using knowledge and logic, but rather by the sensations that arise when the memory is "touched". It is the sensations we measure when considering the SUD. Her SUD when we actually touched it was 8. If we were to refer to this memory based on the importance the client gave it at first, we would miss its big contribution to her sensations today, and miss the opportunity to process it, thereby to improve her condition.

Despite the fact that the client does not think so at first, the impact of a certain memory that gets a SUD score of more than 3 or 4 when actually touched means that it is still impacting him in the present. As the processing takes place, and the influence of the event becomes clear, the client can see its effect on different aspects in life. I hear statements from clients who felt that the past memory was insignificant at first say things like, "This really reminds me of what I'm going through today. I didn't notice it before".

Two mechanisms contribute to the processing going on during therapy. The first is routing the concentration in two parallel channels — "then" and "now". The second is working in such a way that will guarantee participation of both brain hemispheres in the process.

In order to make sure that both hemispheres take part in the processing, there is a need to use a stimulus that will work on both parts of the body and therefore on both parts of the brain. This can be achieved using various methods, such as playing different sounds intermittently in the right and left ears, following an object moving from right to left, etc. I usually use a dedicated EMDR device composed of two small hand-held objects that can vibrate. Sometimes a client comes to me and reports feeling emotional discomfort in his chest, but he does not know why. I have him pick up the two vibrating objects, and within a few sets he knows why because the bilateral stimulus helps connect the body sensation hemisphere and the cognition hemisphere.

During processing, the client is told to let his mind lead him so that he is just observing what is happening and not trying to control it. The associations related to the processed event can take him forward or backward in time, to the different aspects of the memory, to additional details of the event that he did not recall, or to information from different channels — including the cognitive, emotional, sensory, and physical. Either way, the client is instructed to watch from the side, without controlling or judging whether the associations are relevant.

In many cases, the client feels that associations unrelated to the incident come up, and later on the connection becomes apparent to him. I remember such a case when working with a young client who suffered from low self-esteem. In one of our sessions, I asked him what he noticed in the last processing set. He replied, "Something totally unrelated. I suddenly saw a big curtain with a bike on it". I asked him not to judge the associations but to just notice them and in the next processing set he remembered an incident that he experienced at age 4. He and his younger sister received a bike, and while she could ride it easily, he could not and fell off. He remembered family members laughing at him, and from that point, the route to low self-esteem was a short one.

It is important to know that the change in SUD is not unidirectional throughout the process. While working with memory processing, the SUD scale reported by the client might go up and might go down. As long as there is a change, the work should continue. In case a client notices no change, the therapist guides the client to a new direction that might complete the processing in a more accurate manner. In many cases, the lack of change, despite changing directions, indicates that the wrong memory is being processed. This means that this memory is based on an even earlier memory that needs to be processed first. This is called a 'feeder memory' when an earlier memory is the basis of the present memory. After completing processing of an event, the SUD goes down to 0 or near 0, the memory connects to positive beliefs 7 or close to 7 on a 1-7 scale, and the body is relaxed.

Once in a while I come across a case in which the SUD went down in the previous session, and went up in the following session. This could usually indicate two possibilities. The first is that there is another active aspect in the memory that needs to be dealt with. For example, the aspect of feeling embarrassment is complete, but the aspect of anger must still be dealt with. The second possibility is, as previously mentioned, that there is a need to locate and reprocess an earlier memory. In most cases, after completing the processing and the SUD of the memory has gone down to 0, it will remain low forever and will not disturb the client in the future.

"I sit and try to think how the treatment benefited me most… trying to specify the different areas in my life that changed thanks to therapy… and I find it hard, not because things didn't change… on the contrary… because so much has changed.

I was in "regular" therapy before and although I found it very effective and felt I got a lot from it, this method made for a very different experience. I think the main issue for me was the ease in which I saw the results in daily life, in a process that almost never comes from a position of thought (e.g. "I'm in such and such situation right now… I'll do this and that…") but from an almost automatic place. I sometimes felt as if I changed the basic wiring of things, and events that in the past might have shaken me, simply didn't affect me anymore and lost their power over me.

I came to therapy for a specific reason, but quickly understood that the events that had brought me to therapy were related to other earlier events that I was not even really aware of. It was explained to me that those events, even years later, might cause me to act and react in a certain way because of their still active status and of not being processed properly. "Returning" to these events, out of a very clear perspective and a system of processing and re-absorbing, (it sounds long and tiring but sometimes happens in an instant, as if the light went on in the room and things begin to look completely different) made things rest in their place and stopped controlling me. I literally remember finishing a session and leaving with a feeling of 'What, could it really be that simple?!' And the answer is YES. It was that simple for me!"

EMDR PROTOCOL —
WHAT HAPPENS IN
THE TREATMENT ROOM

The work plan in EMDR focuses on three time periods:

A. Past incidents that are stored unprocessed thus created the problem.
B. The symptoms and effects of these memories in the present — present triggers
C. The desired future in the field under focus.

The process is detailed in a protocol built of eight steps:

1. History-taking. Background and "capsules" — locating traumatic memories that still influence the client in the present, on which the treatment program is based. In addition data is collected on present symptoms and triggers, desired goals, and coping resources.

2. Preparation. Content and duration of the preparation stage changes from person to person, depending on the cause of referral and the ability to cope. There are clients for whom the first two stages take 30 minutes, and others who have undergone a serious trauma, or a battery of events with a cumulative impact, who need a longer preparation period. In quite rare cases, such as tough addictions or dissociative disorders, these stages can last weeks or months.

During the preparation stage, the therapist explains to the client the basics of EMDR and what the therapy will be like, and also makes sure that the client has enough coping resources to help him in completing the events' processing. When high functioning people are concerned (working/learning, living their daily lives and not being idle), this is usually a sign that there are already enough resources to allow the client to be able to process. The therapy can then begin. If the person is run-down and cannot function, focus is put on adding coping resources until he can begin processing.

3. Assessment. Information is collected regarding the event that will be the focus of therapy at this stage of the treatment program. These details include an image which represents the sensory and visual channel of the memory, negative words that come with it, positive words that the client would like to come with it after the event is processed, just how much the desired positive words fit as of now with the memory (on a scale of 1-7), what emotions arise when faced with the memory, just how much the memory disturbs the client right now when it is recalled (on a scale of 0 to 10 - These are the measurements known as subjective units of disturbance (SUD) mentioned earlier), and where in the body the memory, or part of it, is felt.

4. Desensitization. In this stage, a completion of the reprocessing of the event is done while activating alternately both brain hemispheres (it is done by eye movements, alternating sounds or alternating tactile/tapping). The desensitization stage lasts until the SUD drops to 0 or near 0. That is, until the memory no longer causes distress in the emotional channel. This step is not in a conversational form, but consists of short sets of silent reprocessing in which the client's brain gets another chance to reprocess the memory that could not be fully processed when it initially happened, along bilateral stimulation of the brain, and short reporting to the therapist. The client is fully awake during the entire procedure. The role of the therapist in this step is to enable the best conditions for reprocessing. The therapist tries to intervene as little as needed as long the reprocessing flows. If it gets stuck the therapist intervenes to make it flow again. The way this step is experienced by clients is different from person to person according to the way their brain is used to coping with difficult material. Some people experience this step as close to "day dreaming", with visual metaphors. Others experience mostly emotional changes of changing perspectives, while others experience the process as a row of insights falling one after another.

5. Installation. In this stage, we verify the completion of processing in the cognitive channel, using the positive desired words. This means that at the end of the installation process, there is a high degree of synchronization between the memory of the incident and the positive words (with the goal of reaching 7, or close to it on a scale of 1-7).

6. Body scan. In this stage, we make sure that there is no residue of the memory remaining that is expressed in the somatic channel of body functions. In case there is such residue, we continue the processing until it disappears.

7. Finishing the processing or finishing the session. This means instructing the client on how to notice what happens after the session, and reporting it to the therapist in the next session.

8. Reevaluation. This stage takes place during the next session or sessions using the SUD scale for the target event, and a short report regarding the impact of the previous processing on daily life. This is in order to make sure that the process has indeed been completed and that there is no need to process further aspects of this target memory.

Where do the memories we work on come from?

When talking about extreme and conspicuous incidents that are at the heart of the distress, there is little difficulty in locating them. However, treating less focused and broader issues, such as problems with self-esteem or problematic patterns with intimate relationships, or with removing "internal blocks" and improving achievements, in most cases the client has some difficulties recognizing what the memories at the core of the blocks are. In this case, sometimes people may mistakenly think that EMDR is not suited for them, since they do not have traumatic memories that haunt them. This misleading notion needs to be corrected. In fact, what "haunts" them is the inability to change their behavior, even though, in theory, they know what needs to be done. The awareness of the behavior that inhibits them does not change it. While in PTSD we can many times recognize the core events as we are also "haunted" by images from those events; in traumatic memories we are "haunted" more by the negative emotions and beliefs in our subconscious, thus it is harder for us to know their origins. Within the first sessions of EMDR, one attains the understanding of the dynamics that cause the block or the pattern, whether by *scanning back* to notice previous events that caused the block, or by *diagnostic EMDR*.

Scanning back. Part of the techniques to locate core events used in therapy can be implemented on one's own as well. However in cases of acute distress, it is strongly recommended not to do so. When it comes to acute events, remembering might increase the level of distress; therefore, it is imperative that in these cases one should seek the help of a therapist trained in treating such events (Criteria for choosing the right EMDR therapist are detailed in Appendix D).

Once we locate a behavior or pattern that is not understood, or that we recognize as causing us stress, and our behavior cannot be explained by present events alone, it is possible to connect to the sensations in three channels:

1. Which emotion goes along with the memory?
2. What negative words go along with it? (A list of common negative beliefs appears in Appendix G).
3. Where do we feel it in the body?

Now we can go back in our memories, find where else we recognize it from, and then make a list. For example, the feeling that I am a loser… Where else do I know that from? Did I feel it in college? If so, when? In high school? When in childhood did I feel it?

Another way of locating key memories is by going chronologically forward. For example, did I feel like a loser in elementary school? Not really, I felt fine, I remember I got along.

So let's go on to middle school. Did I feel like a loser in middle school? And so forth. This chronological advancing allows us to identify the specific points where it began.

Diagnostic EMDR. When there is a difficulty diagnosing the problem, it is possible to work on the last event in which the client acted in a way he had trouble explaining. While processing, we can check what associations this incident connects to. From there, we can begin to explore what is at the heart of the behavior, and reach earlier memories. From this point and on, it is possible to prepare a therapy plan that includes the key events, and progress systematically.

Side Effects

EMDR has three possible side effects:

Feeling tired during or right after the session. This is the most common, but does not always take place and is a natural result of the intensive and multi-dimensional processing being undertaken in EMDR sessions which involves emotional, sensorial, cognitive and somatic elements.

An increase in distress before a decrease is felt. This possible side effect also does not always happen. The processing of a traumatic incident memory usually takes between 1-3 sessions. If the processing was not completed in one session, in some cases, the content of the memory might interfere until the next session (more thoughts and dreams about the event). For this reason, during the preparation stage, the therapist checks whether a client can relax himself before processing begins. Usually, when serious events are involved, I suggest having a double session, or more than one session a week, to minimize the time in between sessions until the work on the event is completed, thereby minimizing or completely eliminating this side effect.

Acting out in the present. This is the rarest of all three, and I have seen it only a few times. It is a situation in which a particularly traumatic event is dealt with, but since the client is confused about whether the feelings and thoughts come from the past or the present, he acts in the present — for example, runs out of the room. I was working with a client who, 10 years prior, had received the bad news that his two-year-old daughter was sick with terminal cancer (which fortunately turned out to be erroneous; the daughter is alive and well today). Once the emotion surfaced, the client ran out of the therapy room even before the session ended. The next day the client returned to complete the processing. It turned out that during the original traumatic moment, when the doctors told him the horrible news, he had an urge to get up and leave the room. When this emotion resurfaced, that is indeed what he did.

Limitations

EMDR is a therapeutic method that, even after many years (since 1987), continues to evolve. For the wider public that does not suffer from severe pathologies, the only limitation is making sure they have sufficient coping resources for processing — which is what is tested and created in the second step of the protocol. For people with more severe disorders there were once some contraindications, but almost all of them were removed at a later point in time after therapists, conducting joint research and clinical work, found ways to circumvent them. This is how EMDR was integrated into treatment for dissociative disorders, people with schizophrenia or bipolar disorders, people with mental retardation, etc.

In addition, the level of training between various EMDR therapists differs. Many limitations presented in the first level of EMDR training are removed after the second more advanced level of training, or with further training and practice.

In certain medical, especially neurological, conditions you should consult your M.D. before starting.

"Over the years, before using EMDR, I had experience with different methods in psychology, psychotherapy, therapy and awareness, etc. The strongest among them was the awareness workshop. Since that point, I tried to find a treatment that would more extensively explore the issues I touched upon via those treatments, including what they were missing; such as delving into the details of my memory, one by one. I knew somewhere that this was the key to the questions I asked myself about the formation of my personality, and once I received answers, I would find the strength for the changes I face in every area of my life.

Due to issues related to a crisis of faith with a therapist I used during my junior year of college (although I did learn some coping techniques), as well as further crises, I was less than excited about seeking out therapy. Most therapists I dealt with made me see myself as less intelligent by "mirroring" little things I did or didn't do throughout the therapy (like not showing up for the session on time), and tried to convince me of its significance. I will not say this is necessarily wrong, but in my case I felt the therapist try to connect this to Freudian ideas and other projections. I spent the rest of my time upgrading my story-telling abilities (which, as I already knew,

I was not bad at). Now I know nothing I experienced had the same emotional effect as EMDR.

Despite the short time I've been treated with EMDR, and my serious fears, on one hand of working on memories (which I have many of and was scared of touching), and on the other hand, of the unusual sounding method (which I didn't know much about), I can definitely say that I haven't felt so vital in years.

I am a beautiful woman, and I've been aware of it since my childhood. The surprising thing is that I only recently started feeling like I deserve to be well-groomed all the time. I used to only groom myself in "waves" and my self-esteem was quite low. The method in which I worked on incidents from my childhood, which I thought was perfect (or at least idyllic and pastoral as a tiny kibbutznik), uncovered something I didn't even remember and brought about an unexpected change…

A flood of visual parts of my earliest memory, enabled through this method (which to my surprise, did not involve hypnosis, but rather consisted of two vibrating balls held in my hand while my eyes were closed), exposed the larger memory to me: When I was little, I lived on a kibbutz. The local children tricked me. They made me swear not to tell any grown up what I ate — a mixture the children made that contained rice from the dining room and probably worms from the ground. This story must have "eaten" me up inside. Remembering it and talking about it caused a change in me. If, in the past, I felt unworthy and could not explain it, suddenly something freed within me, and I changed.

This early punishment through the stomach must have taught me to "keep it inside" and restrain myself when it came to self-

expression, because I could not tell anyone what happened (I promised!). Immediately afterwards, and for many years after, I suffered from stomach aches, which I attributed to growing pains, as well as to genetics or something like that… I completely repressed the real reason.

After this session, I was able to free myself from the memory of my many stomach aches (and the recurring stomach aches), and the old innocent promise to myself (not to let anybody know about the bad things that happened to me), and choose what is best for myself. Ever since then, I feel something significant has changed in my relationship with myself. Recently, I feel like I can communicate with myself better. In addition, I suddenly love and embrace the little girl within, whom I feel to this day is an essential part of who I am. Something I had lost over 20 years ago suddenly returned. I feel more beautiful and confident.

I think it happened because the little girl who kept the secret and covered up for the children, felt really bad about herself and thought this was what she was supposed to feel. Upon being freed from this exhausting duty, years of insecurity were dropped and new vitality and freedom appeared. This allowed the young woman (me!) to feel she had the right to express herself and be herself, and these things finally appear in my natural beauty".

CHAPTER 3

LETTING GO OF THE PAST

Problems masquerading as other problems

Josh

Josh, in his forties, went to therapy on the advice of a friend. His wife had cheated on him and he was left circling the wagon for several months, unsure if he should get divorced or not. His thoughts stumbled between worrying about his kids and their financial stability after a divorce, and between staying with the uncertainty of maintaining a relationship with someone untrustworthy. These thoughts swirled around in his head for several months, along with the unsuccessful stab at conventional psychological counseling.

At the same time, his mental state continued deteriorating. He suffered from insomnia, had health issues, and lack of concentration at work, which added a fear of being fired to the mix.

It was obvious that Josh's problem was not whether to get divorced or not, but rather being strong enough to choose. The real problem was Josh's inability to make a decision, stand behind it, and face the consequences of that decision.

Therefore, the primary therapeutic goal for Josh was not the need to make a decision, but to make him strong enough to make a decision and deal with the consequences. After three sessions that dealt with the current acute crisis, Josh began sleeping well again. Over the next few weeks we used EMDR on a range of events, which had left him in the past with a feeling of weakness, of being led by others, and not being good enough. Josh had a lot of coping powers, so with each passing session we managed to work on one or two incidents from his past.

We processed the comparisons his family used to do between him and his little sister, his being cross-eyed at a young age and getting made fun of for it, as well as issues ranging from his mother having led him without listening to him, to the romantic failures he experienced. Josh told me that he emerged from every session feeling like he was 'standing up straighter' than the session before.

Three months after the therapy began, Josh by chance, met his wife's former lover. Instead of shriveling up as on previous occasions, he told him "Thanks!" and kept walking with his head held high. As a result of therapy, Josh no longer felt weak, and today is able to make a decision and face its consequences. He was no longer willing to live a life of humiliation and disrespect, and subsequently filed for divorce.

Arnold

Arnold, a 45-year-old man, came to therapy with a problem that, he thought, required only a short session or two about his dilemma: Whether or not to have an affair. Before we started dealing with his future relationship, I questioned him about the current one. He described a difficult relationship with his wife, one filled with mutual disrespect, contempt, and even verbal abuse, on both sides. When I asked him to describe the relationship from its onset, I discovered that even then, before they married, it had been a difficult one.

I then asked him if he ever noticed and knew where the red lights were in the past, and if so, why had he not stopped this ride?

While answering my question, it turned out that Arnold had a long history of low self-esteem. I therefore offered an alternative therapeutic goal. Instead of solving the proposed dilemma regarding a mistress, we should begin changing the feeling of inferiority feeling which he had that "beggars cannot be choosers".

Although EMDR therapy usually requires one to three sessions to establish a therapeutic plan, we quickly located the sources of Arnold's problem, and began processing early experiences of mocking by other children, neglect and familial abuse, and a constant feeling of guilt. As the processing progressed, we reached answers to the real relevant questions. They were not whether he should have an extramarital affair, but instead, "What kind of life do I want for myself? Who do I want to share it with? What kind of relationship do I want with them?"

Worth knowing

Many times people approach therapy when they feel stuck in a certain place, without understanding the reason for it. This is because, for many people "the problem hides". In other words, what the person thought was troubling him was, in fact, not the actual problem. Therefore, when trying to solve the wrong problem, the attempt is in vain.

For example, people who are immersed in contemplating an important decision often come to me. The contemplation is hard, and the thought haunts them. They invest many hours of worry without the ability to decide. In most cases, a short inquiry shows that the present dilemma is the result of a deeper reason, for instance, the fear of making a mistake. When that fear does not exist, the ability to try one solution or another and decide later becomes possible. Or feeling an inability to trust one's self. "If I cannot trust myself, how can I trust a decision I'll make?" Or, as in Josh's case, the lack of belief in dealing with the consequences of the choice.

When we correctly define the problem, we can locate the collection of experiences that caused it. Once processing is complete, the "tangle" is released.

How can we know if it is the problem or only a symptom? We check what is happening in other areas of the person's life.

Nancy
Nancy, in her twenties, sought a short counseling session to help her decide who she was attracted to more — men or women? I asked her to describe how she made other important decisions in her life, for example, school. She replied, "Funny you should ask, because I'm really having a hard time deciding between university and college". It became clear that the present deliberation was not about a particular area of her life, but rather about the fear of making a mistake. After working on this fear, Nancy realized that deciding between men or women did not matter to her, and she did not have to make a decision in advance.

Breakups and divorce

Eva
Eva, a 27-year-old, came to therapy after her boyfriend broke up with her. It was her first serious relationship, as they had been together since she was 18. Prior to the breakup there had been a few months of deterioration in the relationship.

When they were on vacation overseas, just before returning home, her boyfriend dumped her. She was in a foreign country, with only the boyfriend who wanted to dump her, and felt distant and disconnected from friends and family. For Eva, this was a traumatic experience, accompanied by shock and surprise, which stayed with her for months afterwards. Her functioning was affected and her feelings of anxiety began to generalize and spread further and further. In the beginning she had a difficult time being in places that reminded her of her ex partner, and later on it spread to an entire geographical area. Finally she avoided visiting the city he lived in as much as possible.

Eva described having never felt such distress in the past, nor the feelings of worthlessness and pessimism that she now experienced. On the contrary, she used to be a very optimistic person with a feeling of self-worth. She felt that the situation had suddenly changed.

We worked on processing meaningful events in the period during which the relationship with her boyfriend deteriorated. The therapeutic work was done based on a specific protocol of EMDR, which is dedicated to events that occurred recently, and are still taking place in the present. Later on, we worked on certain "triggers" in the present that caused her anxiety and avoidance. Afterwards, we focused on the future and her ability to meet her ex-boyfriend without feeling such distress, and, of course, to start dating other men. After several sessions, Eva rid herself of her generalized anxiety and could return to the places she had avoided. The all therapy lasted a few months. Afterwards, she was able to see her ex-boyfriend without feeling distressed, and search for a different healthy relationship.

Worth knowing
Post-traumatic symptoms such as restlessness, terrifying thoughts, nightmares, flashbacks, and avoidance are not just the results of life-threatening traumas like accidents, terror attacks, or serious illnesses. The same symptoms can appear after difficult emotional situations. Difficult emotional situations that are overwhelming for us in real time (because they are strong or because we are young, weak, ill, surprised) can also get stored dysfunctionally in our brain in their 'raw' state.

After a breakup, people sometimes have the misconception that therapy has no point if it cannot bring back their partner. This, too, is a case of wrong conceptualization of the problem. Breakups are common events and despite the fact that they can cause great pain, most people manage to pull through. Usually, when someone cannot function after a breakup, the problem is not that he "was dumped", but his diminished capacity to go on. This can be the result of depression, but also of negative beliefs such as "Nobody wants me", or "I cannot trust anyone", formed from past experiences. Within the framework of therapy, the past experiences and negative messages caused by them, can definitely be identified and processed properly, thereby getting rid of those feelings.

Eric

Eric came to me after his wife betrayed him. She actually did not cheat on him with another man, but rather betrayed his confidence by writing a blog where she shared intimate details without telling it to him. Whenever he thought about what had happened, and despite attempts to forgive her and move on, he could not stop experiencing the same feelings at the moment of discovery. He experienced "flashbacks" and intrusive thoughts and felt that despite wanting to move on, he simply could not do so. Together, via our therapy session, we processed the moment of discovery. Similar to any other traumatic memory, after the processing finished, the same feelings stopped haunting him. They became a thing of the past, instead of an ever-present event, and he and his wife managed to continue onward and rebuild their relationship.

Worth knowing

When there is cheating by one member of the couple, it can be processed by EMDR. The processing does not necessarily guarantee that the couple will stay together, or that they feel indifference in case the relationship ends. The meaning of processing is to ensure that the difficult emotions brought about via the deterioration of the relationship, and the betrayal or separation, no longer haunt the client. The results include: no longer having obsessive thoughts about them, no longer experiencing flashbacks, and no longer having the emotions haunt them with the same intensity. Under these conditions, even if they choose to separate, decisions can be made reasonably. For example, when children are involved, this allows for a more comfortable separation process that can more easily result in joint custody.

I sometimes encounter people who either did not go to therapy during their divorce proceedings, or attempted the standard talk therapy which, unfortunately, only stayed with their pain while the situation got worse. People hired expensive lawyers and paid huge sums of money, just so they can get back at their partner. Proper therapy with EMDR can usually prevent this turmoil and bring about a state where even meetings between ex-partners and new partners are possible, and not accompanied by feelings of humiliation and insult.

I often see the long-term effects that divorce has on children. These same children can turn out to be 30-40-year-old adults that reach my practice, but the effects are still apparent. Many times, the negative impacts do not stem from the divorce itself, rather from a childhood with parents who didn't get along, or from the exposure to parents who suffered great pain in front of their young children. These situations can create for the children a feeling that they cannot burden their parents. It can also be parents who said something bad about the other parent, or a parent who told his or her children, "If it were not for you, I would have put a bullet through my head". Such children grow up to be adults lacking the feeling of a safe home. All such experiences can cause the children to have negative beliefs about themselves and about the world, and continue to impact them. EMDR therapy can change such beliefs.

Brick by brick — a memory feeding other memories

According to the model that guides the work in EMDR, things that bother us in the present stem from past events that were not completely processed in real-time. In addition, many times they are stacked one atop the other when the memories of previous events feed off later memories.

Roy

Roy, a 35-year-old homosexual man, lived with his partner. He "came out" to his mother and brother, but was very frightened to tell his father. He thought the problem was his sexual orientation. In this case it was not only a wrong conceptualization, but also a trapping one.

Further insights led Roy to understand that the issues preventing him from telling his father about his sexual orientation were, amongst other things, fear of being different, shame in sexuality, a desire to protect his father and an actual fear of his own father. Memories related to fear of being different were connected to kindergarten and a stuttering problem that caused him to be ostracized by other kids. Negative associations with sexuality were related to early memories of masturbating and getting caught by his parents, and this led him to associate sexuality with shame. Another reason was the worry that this news would hurt his father's health, as his father had dealt with a heart attack in the recent past. Roy had not processed the event of his father's heart attack properly, and still felt that any small incident could hurt him. Finally, the last reason was the fear of angering his father, as memories in which his father exploded in anger, and threw things at various family members, when Roy was young, were still fresh in his mind. These issues were addressed in therapy, with the goals of being able to locate the key events in those areas, and complete the necessary processing. Eventually, after several sessions processing the memories, Roy felt more comfortable sharing his sexual orientation.

Sharon

Sharon, 30 years old, came to therapy due to difficulties in romantic relationships. We began by working on her first relationship, at age 12, with a boyfriend who dumped her. She felt that the experience had left her with a feeling of very low self-worth. As she told me, "How did this boy, even at age 12, already know that I am not worthy? He didn't even break up with me, but sent a friend to do it instead". After working on this early memory with her successfully, I felt that there were even earlier memories which attributed to this feeling of low self-worth. I explained to her that she wrongly connected the break-up to an issue related to her value, when instead, she could have thought,

"Wow, we were 12, look at how infantile he was, he could not even break up with me himself", or "Look at the jerk. What a coward, he could not even approach me on his own".

We needed to work on the earliest memories that made her feel unworthy. This feeling played out in her future relationships.

We worked on several earlier events connected to this feeling, in comparison to her younger brother and older sister. In fact, the earlier feelings of unworthiness led to the 6th grade breakup affecting her so severely. They created a situation in which the breakup only validated those negative feelings. Once these roots were properly processed, later romantic relationships were much easier to tackle.

Rachel

Rachel, a 40-year-old woman on her second marriage, came to me because of stress in the relationship with her husband. In addition, she mentioned feelings of constant guilt in their interactions as well. The complex part of the therapy was not solving the feelings of stress and guilt, but convincing her to process a memory from age 3, which came up during the first session. The memory involved a visit to the planetarium. She became startled and started to cry, and her parents took her out and shouted at her. She remembered very clearly the strong feeling of guilt she then felt. After processing a memory that she had been carrying around for almost 40 years, the feeling of guilt that she experienced every time she was reprimanded was lifted. She returned to her partner without the constant feelings of guilt, and her relationship improved.

Worth knowing

Since EMDR is such an effective method, many times the difficult part is not the processing itself, but rather, explaining to people the need to return to a younger age to retrieve memories. The events that make up the core of many problems tend to occur at a very young age for two reasons. Firstly when we are younger, we tend to think that everything has to do with us. A child might think to himself, "Why is Dad yelling? I must be doing something wrong". The child does not have the capacity to wonder if maybe the boss annoyed Dad, or Dad is upset with Mom, or worried about financial issues, etc. This means, that as kids, we attribute what is going on around us to ourselves. Secondly, as children, we have fewer resources; therefore many things that happen to us are overwhelming. As adults we can handle the event, but when it occurred, we could not; thus a traumatic memory was created. The beauty in EMDR is that the client knows what to do with these early memories. Instead of thinking, "Ok, I'm screwed up because of a something from my childhood", we now know that we can rewind and complete the processing of the events that left us with negative impressions, and change the symptoms and their impact.

People are sometimes surprised by the memories that come up, since they did not attribute such importance to them. In

EMDR, we use the SUD test to decide whether a memory warrants our attention. The score ranges from 0-10, where 0 represents a neutral event, one that the client remembers peacefully (after all, remembering something is ok, amnesia is not desired), while 10 represents a troublesome and truly disturbing memory. When we check the SUD score of a certain incident, we are checking whether the incident is active or not. If the event is active, it surely has an impact on life in the present. If the impact is not known in the beginning of therapy, it becomes apparent during therapy.

Alan

Alan, 24, a very thin man, came to me after losing a lot of weight, yet still perceived himself as fat. In order to change this perception, we utilized EMDR to locate the incidents that "burned" him with the sensation of being physically flawed. The memories we tackled were ones in which kids made fun of him in school, of sweating in school, and eating in secret. Another memory was one in which he would eat two falafels while other kids ate only half.

Neil

When Neil came to me, he was still fat as the result of emotional eating and self-punishment. We located and processed an early childhood memory in which he overheard his mother sharing a story with his older sister of Neil standing on a table at a very young age, and breaking it. The story left him with the feeling of being fat and therefore flawed from an early age, and this was still the feeling he had when I first met him. We worked on that memory, and since eating was a comfort for his body loathing, many of his obsessions regarding food disappeared.

Worth knowing:

Sometimes experiences relating to anxiety and stress cause stomachaches. This is because during stressful situations one of the systems impacted is the digestive system. The blood leaves it in favor of the emergency system. As a result, during stress, there can be stomachaches, nausea and even diarrhea and vomiting. The situation can cause a feeling of "having a hole in the stomach". It can feel like the feeling of actual hunger, while actually those feelings stem from stress, fear, or emotional pain. Such a feeling, in turn, can lead to emotional eating to ease this emotional pain.

Abe

Abe suffered from low self-esteem and low self-confidence. Despite suffering ridicule and being picked on by kids in school, the source of the low self-worth was even earlier than that. From the time he was young until he was 16, he suffered physical abuse from his father. When he was 16 and physically bigger than his father, he confronted him and threatened to retaliate. His father stopped beating him but continued abusing him verbally. As we kept working on the early experiences of violence and degradation at home, Abe's self-worth improved dramatically.

Worth Knowing:

Traumatic memories can be linked to one another, while being kept separate from the adaptive general memory network. Therefore, if the case is of prolonged suffering, such as daily violence, there is no need to review hundreds of memories, but only a select few, of which their processing influences the processing of other similar memories.

Dead end

People might still struggle between possible solutions to a problem, since no solution seems appropriate. But there are options they may have not yet considered.

Eli

When I asked Eli, a 45-year-old, what I could do for him, he replied that he didn't believe that the problem from which he suffered could be solved. I accepted the challenge. He said, "Look, for several years now I have been spending most of my nights in the following way: I sit on the balcony, smoke a cigarette, and wonder if the kids I had with my wife are not really mine. I suspect my wife cheated on me, and they are not my biological kids, but I will never get a DNA test. I do not want to cause them problems with being bastards, etc., and see no other option except spending my evenings sitting on the porch, smoking a cigarette and wondering". We went back in time to examine the events that caused Eli to suspect his wife. We located a memory from college, when he and his wife met. It turns out that he read a book at the time about a woman who was sexually distant from her husband, who was also cheating on him with many other men. This idea entered his head and took hold.

After processing this memory, Eli remembered the time when the gynecologist gave them an estimate of when his wife became pregnant. In both pregnancies, it was when he was overseas. However, he also remembered that even then he looked into the matter and found that the dating system of the doctor is not 100% accurate, and could be wrong by a few days. In other words, there was no actual validation to the suspicion that the children were not his. Managing this problem, which went on for years, took three sessions. After processing memories of the book and the doctor giving the time frame while he was overseas, Eli got back the sense that his kids were his own, without the need for DNA testing. He no longer spent time on the porch, thinking those same old disturbing thoughts.

Worth knowing

In a similar way, clients sometimes tell me, "I have a huge mortgage and if I get fired I will have no way of paying it back, therefore I have nothing to do but to live with the constant fear of being fired". In such instances, using EMDR, immunity to anxiety can be developed. The anxiety will not, of course, prevent you from being fired. On the contrary, since it disturbs your functioning, it might lead to it. What could help dealing with the anxiety, however, is the belief that one can cope even in face of adverse situations. The feeling that even if fired, you will not fail. One has to believe that he can deal with it and find a new job. EMDR can be used to work on a sense of stability and security through processing of early memories of what damaged this sensation, and created that feeling of, "I am weak, I cannot deal, and I'm hopeless".

Leo

Leo, a 25-year-old man, came to me with a very serious depression. It was so severe that he had already attempted to take his own life by strangulation. At the last minute, he removed the noose from around his neck, went to see a psychiatrist who recommended therapy. In the first few sessions, when asked, "How are you?" the answers were, "Too bad I didn't die in a terror attack", and "Too bad I was not run over by a truck".

He attributed his depression to his homosexuality, but since he believed the problem was something that would never change, he led himself to a literal dead end. He thought "If I am depressed for a reason that will not go away, I have no alternative but to continue suffering". We had to change the conceptualization of the problem. Being gay does not necessitate depression at all, thus the problem was the actual depression and not the sexual orientation. Depression can be manageable in therapy — and thus hope finally seemed reasonable.

Leo had quite a few incidents that were at the core of his depression. His parents' difficult divorce and the sexual exploitation he had gone through. After working on them systematically, he no longer felt suicidal.

Worth Knowing

In order to work with EMDR, one needs basic reprocessing resources and strength. EMDR can be used alongside medication to treat acute depression not brought on by a traumatic incident. While waiting for the medication to kick in, EMDR can be used to raise strengths and access certain resources by raising events from the past with which the client had managed to deal well. After a period of strengthening, EMDR is then used to work on past events.

As was the case with Leo, when there is a severe depression, the person can act and feel as though he is on a downward spiral. In other words, the client feels as though going to school or work is pointless because his destiny has already been determined. Practically, not studying new things will lead to dead end jobs that will lead nowhere, with no hope of advancement, where he will be treated badly, and feel as if he has no way out.

However, when one begins to feel hope and optimism, an opening appears, and one can start planning for the future. He can go to school, find a more challenging job, and begin to feel life turn around.

Aiming low

Many times people who come to me aim too low; they mistakenly think that the inhibition stopping them is objective and independent, but actually, the psychological aspect contributes as well.

Ariel

Ariel, age 29, came to see me. He explained his problem as such: "Look, I have a learning disability in English, and that's why I could not finish my high school exams. Except for English, it is all done, and now I've decided to finish English as well. I signed up for night school, but it is really hard; I cannot seem to even open up the English study book. I open it and close it right away". He begged me, and expressed his future eternal gratitude, if I could help him at least pass the test.

I worked backwards with Ariel using an EMDR technique called "Float Back". This technique connects you to the sensations of the memory through several channels — cognitive, emotional and physical, and allows you to locate the time when the initial contributing event took place.

We arrived at a kindergarten memory, in which Ariel had learnt to write his name in English and Hebrew. In Hebrew he wrote it correctly, but felt humiliated when the teacher laughed at him for writing it incorrectly in English. After spending two sessions finalizing the processing of that memory, Ariel could open the English book and continue learning. Within just a few weeks, he advanced and could already sit and study for hours. A few months later, I received a call in which Ariel let me know that he aced the test. His grade? 95!

John

John came to see me because of issues relating to lack of self-confidence and the inability to make decisions. During one of our sessions, he requested that we take a break to focus instead on his upcoming SAT test, and his difficulty with the math portion. Every time he encountered a math problem he could not solve, he felt his brain turn to rubber and was unable to concentrate.

We returned to using the same Float Back technique to identify incidents that created a fear of mathematics. We found two such memories. The first was a memory from kindergarten in which an incident during playtime led him to feel stupid and incapable of understanding anything. The second was an incident in elementary school where a harsh comment from a teacher after a bad grade left him feeling bad. Although John's math skills did not suddenly, magically appear, after processing the memories, he was able to spend time on the math problems and solve them. He no longer felt as if his brain was made of rubber, and no longer felt anxious. As a result of those three sessions, John scored higher and higher on the math portion of the SAT. Now that he could cope without running away from the difficulty, the results were astounding: He scored in the highest 2%.

Worth knowing

When people tell me of a particular learning disability that they feel they have, or say, "That's just the way it is; I'm not good at math". I explain that although it is possible that there is an objective component to the difficulty, there is usually a psychological component that can be treated. After dealing with it, we can then see what part of the difficulty still remains. Often, learning disabilities are accompanied by a history of failures that cause feelings of anxiety and wrong assumptions, which on their own can definitely impact learning abilities.

Awareness is overrated

Aaron

Aaron came to see me after walking through life feeling as if he is a disturbance to everyone around him. He didn't feel comfortable asking his wife for anything "since it might disturb her". At work, he never approached his boss in case "he might be disturbing him". He even avoided returning phone calls in case "it might disturb them if I call right now". He had participated in some self-awareness classes and knew exactly how it all started, but did not know what to do with this knowledge. Being aware did not change anything.

The memory that he recalled was being aged 4, lying in bed, and calling for his mother to come. His father arrived and slapped him for yelling, "Stop disturbing!" he screamed at him. Terrified, he wet his bed and did not even let his parents know. This incident caused a connection between a big sense of fear and the feeling that he is a nuisance. This meant that every time Aaron thought he might be disturbing someone, the thought appeared together with great anxiety that something bad was about to happen. After spending two sessions completing the processing of this event, accompanied by many abreactions (Abreaction is an emotional outlet that allows the client to free himself of the emotional experience which accompanies the traumatic memory), Aaron no longer walked around feeling that he was always in everyone's way.

Worth knowing

When touching on those unprocessed memories characterized by being kept separate from the general memory network, the content of the given age in which they were created, arises, together with the level of logic of that age, and abreactions may occur. A 30-year-old, when referencing a memory from age 6, can tell me, "I'm a bad man for having stolen the apple from the neighbor". Processing this memory might lead him to think differently, such as, "It is just an apple, why did I even take it seriously?"

A 40-year-old man might break into tears and think, "I cannot believe it. I broke the vase grandma loved so much!" when, in fact, he is referring to a memory from age 7. Processing the memory might lead him to think, "It is just a vase, and it was not intentional". Before processing, the content appears in the same form that it was experienced in the original incident, with the perspective and awareness of that age. A 40-year-old client burst into tears upon processing the roots of feelings of weakness and not being good enough. He remembered experiencing feelings of humiliation and degradation, when at age 3 he was dressed identically to his 2 year old brother, giving everyone the impression that they were twins. These feelings stayed with him for 35 years. Letting them go required only one session of processing.

Leah

Leah came to me at the age of 30 after 15 (!) years of therapy, including Psychodynamic therapy, Cognitive therapy and so on. She thought she had tried it all. Some of the therapies were neutral at best and some only made her condition worse. She had an ongoing pattern of painful relationships, which the various therapies did not prevent from taking place. A number of therapists suggested that her behavior was the result of sexual abuse that she could not remember. This only made it harder for her and increased her distress. In fact, she was not a victim of sexual abuse that she could not remember. However, she could remember some hurtful incidents in an earlier stage of her life. In her case as well as in many others, being aware of these incidents changed very little. Finally processing them, however, made a huge impact. What Leah could not do in 15 years — with much agony — she managed to achieve in just a few months of EMDR, with an ever-growing sense of relief.

Worth knowing

Fifteen years is not the record for most time in therapy I have heard of. There are those who are in therapy for much longer. The record among the clients I met is 25 years of previous therapies. When the standard therapy does not work, the clients might reach the unfortunate conclusion that all forms of therapy are useless, or that they are a lost cause. This is not true! There are ways to know whether one is undergoing successful therapy (Criteria for knowing if you are getting successful therapy are in Appendix F). One of my clients had been going to therapy, on and off, for 17 years before coming to me. In those years every week he would cry on his therapist's shoulder, experience some relief… until the next week. And this cycle went on and on. I personally do not believe in therapy that only offers a short measure of relief, a therapy that its effect does not even last more than a week, and neither should you. It is worthwhile working on problems from the root and fixing them.

People who have tried other methods for improving awareness in their lives, such as personal growth seminars, coaching and other kinds of therapy, work faster at times with EMDR, since they are already aware of the incidents that affected them. Unfortunately, awareness on its own is not enough to initiate change. With EMDR one can make the extra move needed to make such a change. These clients come ready with a "list of incidents" that can be processed systematically.

What about those who do not know when their suffering began in the present? Awareness is not a precondition for therapy. It is possible to locate the memories using a simple technique. In such cases, we usually need one to three sessions to build a therapeutic program by making a chronological list of key memories that lead to distress or inhibition in the present.

More unfortunate connections

Jacob

Jacob, a client in his 30's, felt that he had a difficult time expressing emotions. We went back and reached a memory from age 7, in which his younger brother fell off a chest of drawers onto the floor. Jacob remembered bursting into tears from the commotion that was created and the agitation that came with it. In response, his father yelled at him to, "Stop crying like a girl!" Ever since, he had found it very difficult to display emotions, since displaying emotions was linked to an unwanted feeling. In other words, the display of an emotion was a "trigger" for those harsh memories to surface. After processing the memory, Jacob started feeling and displaying his emotions in a more liberated manner.

Ruthie

With Ruthie, a divorcee in her 40's, a very unfortunate connection was also formed. A year ago she remembered having an erotic dream while napping on the couch. She awoke to the ringing of the phone, and the receipt of very bad news about a family member's passing. This situation that happened when she was off guard and sleepy caused a connection between sexual feelings and thoughts, and anxiety, and led to the situation in which every time she felt sexually aroused the feeling was accompanied by anxiety. Vice-versa, every time she was anxious she also felt sexually aroused. These two triggers, sexual arousal and feelings of anxiety, brought Ruthie's unprocessed, raw, traumatic memory to the surface, which included the emotions, thoughts and bodily feelings from the moment the unprocessed memory occurred.

Solutions and "solutions"

It is better to notice when the solution is temporary and when it is a solution to the source of the problem.

Zak

Zak, 24 years old, came to therapy and claimed to have a very difficult problem, which was out of his control. Two or three times a week he would look for a one-night stand with a stranger online. He did not even really enjoy it and therefore could not understand what motivated him to do so. Even worse, he felt that by encountering these men, he was putting himself at risk because he might become a victim of sexual assault. Despite this, Zak could not get rid of the urge to continue.

At the first session, I instructed him to notice exactly what happened to him before going online — meaning, what kind of thought, situation or dynamic occurred before this happened each time. He came back the following week and mentioned two things he had noticed. The first one was the feeling of, "I am unlovable", which gave him the urge to go online and look for a one-night stand. The second was that he would do so after every fight with his mother.

We started tracking the sources of his feelings of being unlovable. We reached a difficult memory from the 4th grade, in which he was ostracized. It was such an unpleasant experience for him that he transferred to another school. Using EMDR, we worked on the memory of being banned by his classmates until it didn't bother him any further. We managed to process the bad memories through his present resources, when he was more socially active and had many friends.

The following week, Zak mentioned having only met one stranger for a one night stand. He felt more in control of his behavior, but still not as much as he had hoped to be. We went to work on the other thing he noticed; the fights with his mother. He mentioned a particularly bad fight with her several years ago, which contributed to the current tension between them. Over the next two sessions we processed the memory of that fight, until the memory was not accompanied by a negative feeling. In the following session, Zak confirmed that he was now in control of his self-destructive behavior, and no longer felt the same urges. To make sure the change was permanent; we set up an appointment in a few weeks' time. Indeed, all was well and we parted ways. I checked up on him two years after having completed therapy and he was still doing well, meeting partners out of will and not out of compulsion.

Zak's entire therapy took six sessions, including one follow-up session.

Worth knowing

In cognitive therapy or in personal growth seminars, the working assumption is that negative beliefs are the problem and therefore one tries to confront them and bring about a change. In EMDR, we assume that the negative beliefs are not the problem but a symptom of a negative incident (or incidents), that was not fully processed in real-time, thus creating this negative beliefs.

Similarly, with Aaron (previously mentioned), the same client who kept feeling that he was a nuisance, the goal was not to teach him to fight against his negative beliefs, or remind himself that those beliefs were wrong, or to change his internal story. Rather, after reprocessing the root of the negative feelings, he got rid of them.

The same process is also true regarding different methods of personal growth that are not considered psychotherapy. In those methods they call it "the judging critic" or the "little voice" or "a paradigm" referring to the negative thoughts that pop into our head and guide our behavior and are the reason for the problem. According to EMDR, those internal voices do indeed cause suffering, but they are perceived as symptoms of an earlier experience, not the problem itself.

In EMDR, we do not work on the past to make it prettier so that we can look back on it with joy. But since the present is influenced by incidents that occurred in the past that still influence us today, we process the past so that the present and future will be better.

Postpartum depression

Susan

Susan, a social worker, came to see me after feeling terrible distress a year and half after giving birth to her son. Since the delivery, she experienced constant fits of anger and frequent crying attacks. As a result, her relationship with her husband had also been damaged and she felt enormous guilt. As a therapy professional herself, Susan was aware of her problems, but could not help herself.

In our first session, we started working by a specific protocol of EMDR for an incident that happened in the past, but also had parts of it that were still happening in the present. Susan described the sequence of events, beginning from the moment before it all started until the present, including thoughts of the future. The goal was to create a narrative on which we could work, and check which events were still "active", i.e., which events continued to cause her distress and make life difficult, in order to complete their processing. That is what we did for the next two sessions.

I have learnt that applying EMDR to therapists-clients usually results in EMDR working at a faster pace than non-therapists clients. Usually, working on a traumatic memory takes one to three sessions. Working with therapists, usually two or sometimes three memories can be processed in one session. With Susan, since she already reported feeling better, we stopped after only three sessions. After therapy was discontinued, she returned for a fourth session, to let me know that she felt normal again; she felt happy being around her child, and her relationship with her husband improved. Susan most likely suffered from postpartum depression and therefore had a few rough months. The mental processing of this period helped her become free of it.

With EMDR, when we speak of emotional processing it does not mean to talk for several hours about a specific memory, but rather complete its processing in a sensory, cognitive, emotional and somatic way. (See Chapter 2 on how EMDR works).

Worth knowing

With many women, postpartum depression may stem not only from hormonal changes but also from traumatic memories from the pregnancy period, from past events (such a natural miscarriage), the birth itself, or from the first few days after birth. These memories can include a feeling of helplessness that does not pass.

A person can be very much aware, successful, and with abundant beneficial experiences. But, as mentioned before, traumatic memories are stored separately from the general memory network and the two parts are not accessible to each other for integration. Despite the fact that the effect of the traumatic memory is not felt at all times and that the client experiences himself or herself to be as successful and healthy, the right "trigger" might raise the stored traumatic memory. As previously mentioned, the content of the memory is kept along with the feelings and emotions that were experienced at the time of the event, and might not be adapted to the client's feelings and emotions today.

Driving anxiety, flying anxiety and other anxieties

Bob

Bob, 25 years old, finished a Bachelor's degree in computer sciences but had a difficult time finding a suitable job. When at last he found one, it required him to commute a long way to work. He did not have the possibility to get to work by public transportation, and had not driven since the army. While in the army, he was driving with other passengers in the car, and had been in a near-fatal accident. This was a traumatic experience for him and he avoided driving. Bob had several additional problems, but the reason he came to therapy was to start driving again and start working to gain experience in his field.

He was a strong man with good coping skills. Since the reason for his avoiding driving was a relatively recent one, therapy was particularly short. We met twice: once to process the memory of the accident in the army, and the other to work on the future. With EMDR, we work on future readiness with a therapeutic protocol built especially for this purpose, in which a client is instructed to imagine situations in the future taking place as he would like them to (This technique is very useful when helping athletes before a competition, musicians before a performance, or business people before requests for a raise or promotion. I will get into more detail in the next chapter). Working with Bob, we focused on his ability to get into a car and drive.

After two sessions, Bob took a refresher driving lesson, which he had previously not been able to do. Since then he has been driving himself to and from work. After three years, I checked up on him. He was still driving and doing well.

Daniel

Daniel, a 30-year-old, told me that he was flying overseas in two weeks to visit family. He mentioned his distaste for flying since he did not react well to it. When asked what he meant by that, he told me that during flights he becomes nauseous and vomits. I ask him if this occurred both when flying to and from Israel. He replied that this only occurred in flights when he returns to Israel.

In order to focus his problem and to be accurate with my diagnosis, I kept asking differentiating questions that would help me in ruling out unrelated options. I asked if he always suffered from this, or only since a specific point in his life. He replied that the feeling only started when he turned 18. Before that, flying had not affected him at all. When we started looking into what had happened at that age, he recalled a memory of making Aliyah (moving to Israel from another country), at a young age, and being placed in a boarding school where he was abused by other boys. When he was 18 and returning to Israel from a visit to Russia, he found one of his abusers on the flight with him. This led him to associate flying with the trauma in his youth and subsequently he developed anxiety.

In the two sessions we had before Daniel's flight, we processed memories of the abuse at the boarding school, and the same traumatic flight from age 18. His fear of flying disappeared. He has flown many times since then, and has not been sick on a flight ever again.

Worth knowing

It is important to see a good therapist, one who knows how to diagnose and treat correctly. With the wrong diagnosis, a therapist would have wounded up taking Daniel's money in vain, filling him up with facts on flying as a safe mode of travel, or charged huge sums of money for talking endlessly about why he only suffers on flights to Israel, etc. Instead, with EMDR, we simply recognized the events, looked at them, and finished processing them. This is how we avoid the possibility of making mistakes with all sorts of unnecessary speculations.

There are cases where the source of flight or driving anxiety is clear. For example, in the case of a particularly rough flight in harsh weather that created the anxiety. In such cases, very few therapeutic sessions are needed for complete recovery.

An acquaintance told me that he suffered from driving anxiety and had been in therapy for the past six years. In order to manage the anxiety, the therapist suggested he memorize the route with a map.

This recommendation resulted in an opposite result and preserved the anxiety, because it created a new anxiety of remembering the route, and it would not allow my acquaintance to cope in case of an unexpected change in the route. When I help people who have driving anxiety, their sense of security does not depend on memorizing a specific route, but rather on their ability to cope in a various ways in a variety of situations. For example, one can use a GPS, stopping and calling for assistance, or asking directions from pedestrians — meaning that the sense of the clients' security is from dealing with actual events and feeling that they themselves can find the solution should they encounter a problem.

There are more complicated cases, in which the anxiety is felt from the first flight or from the first attempt at driving. In such cases, the anxiety is a symptom of another problem that is expressed in driving, or while flying.

Gil

Gil came to therapy due to problems with intimate relationships. In one of the sessions he mentioned his concern over a flight he would be taking in two days' time. Since the first time he flew, he always experienced a feeling that death was imminent. We searched for the source of the "I am about to die" feeling, accompanied by anxiety in Gil's past, and came across a memory from when he was four years old. He mentioned that his religious parents had spoken to him about resurrection of the dead. Thus the thought of dying, his parents dying, and even worse — the image of them rising from the dead — filled him with terror. He remembered crying and having a very hard time relaxing. Working on the memory made it easier for Gil on the next flight.

Sean

Sean experienced a fear of flying ever since his first flight. He shared with me that while on the plane, his thoughts were: "The plane is about to fall and we are all going to die". While looking for the source of the fear, he remembered a class trip in the 4th grade during which he endured a near-death experience when he almost fell off a high cliff and told himself that he was going to die. He was saved by the guard who accompanied the trip, but noticed during the processing the years he had spent avoiding travelling, writing it off as "Just not feeling like it". Processing the memory made it easier for him to fly.

Ella

Ella, 29 years old, came to therapy after a series of panic attacks. She had a very active anxiety disorder. She arrived to my practice dressed in pajamas and slippers, having not gone to work for several days, and sleeping at relatives instead of at her own home. After several preliminary questions aimed at making sure she had enough resources for therapeutic work I began working with her. Our work was based on an EMDR variation for a continuing event that has not yet finished. After the first session, she relaxed and returned to work.

That same week, we met for a second session, and afterwards she was able to return home. In acute circumstances, to avoid further deterioration in the situation, and bring about improvement, we can and should meet with a therapist more than once a week.

Worth knowing

One of the differences between EMDR and other psychological methods is the way one views the root of the problem. I'll give an example from an Israeli reality show. One of the participants was a large man who feared dogs because he was bitten by one at a young age. Another participant was a blind man who used a seeing-eye dog, so there was no choice but to get used to the presence of a dog. Slowly the fear did subside, and he eventually walked the dog and petted it.

When the participant left the show, the hosts commented, "Look at how great this is. You stopped fearing dogs. So what do you think? Will you get a dog now?" He replied, "Are you nuts?! I'm terrified of dogs. That specific dog was OK, but other dogs?!" This interaction from the show is a perfect example of how treating the phobia only by exposure to the anxiety inducing object, and attempting to get used to its presence, does not rid us of the underlying fear. Namely following constant exposure under certain circumstances the fear can be managed, but when those circumstances change, the anxiety can come back, as the traumatic content at the root of this symptom has not yet been processed.

Sexual performance anxiety

Nick

After Nick divorced, he was surprised to find that he suffered from sexual performance issues with his new sex partners, something which made him very distraught. During the session, we realized that Nick perceived sex as a test, which instead of inducing passion, induced anxiety. He realized that in the past, he had thought of himself as "not good enough" and therefore must prove himself. EMDR processing of several events that contributed to this feeling (negative incidents with his ex-wife, failure in other aspects of life), together with working on other later events specifically related to his sexual functioning (recent memories of problems with sexual function that, on their own, created a vicious circle of anxiety) allowed the problem to pass in just a few sessions, and never return.

Worth knowing

In my experience with young men who came to therapy for sexual performance problems, I strongly recommend they not use medications when the problems stem from performance anxiety. This is a short-term solution that perpetuates the anxiety. The client becomes emotionally dependent on the pill and is afraid that if he does not use it, he will not be able to function; this anxiety, leads to sexual difficulties the next time he tries to perform without a pill.

In the clinic, I come across two types of performance anxiety. In the first, the man functions well, but only becomes anxious regarding sexual functioning. In such cases, we work on those events and the problem is solved in just a few sessions, without the need for medication. In the second, the client tells of anxiety that impacts his functioning in more fields, but bothers him most in his sexual functioning. This anxiety is rooted deeper in his past and not necessarily related to sex, but is expressed during sexual function — for example, the feeling of, "I must be the best" or "If I am not perfect, I will be abandoned", which then manifests in his sexual function. This triggers pressure and tension. In such cases, more time is required than the first situation; but not long term therapy.

Nora

Nora, 25 years old, suffered from recurrent nightmares of a sexual nature from an early age. She was treated from age 15 with several methods of therapy, part of which made her condition worse as some therapists told her that her symptoms were probably a result of a sexual assault she did not remember. Recalling those nightmares brought up an experience from her childhood in which her mother took her to the doctor for fear of having worms. The exam took place in front of her mother and younger brothers, and although she attempted to resist the checkup, she remembered having the doctor force her to go through with it.

The processing of the event took two sessions. In the first, we worked on the feelings of humiliation and in the second, worked on the feeling of helplessness that she felt. After processing, Nora told me that not only did her dreams no longer contain sexual nightmares, but were now positive and desired sexual dreams.

Tantrums/Fits of rage

Max's wife threatened to leave him unless he worked on his tantrums, since she was no longer able to tolerate them. Rick's boss threatened to fire him, despite respecting his professionalism, the next time he threw a tantrum at work. In both cases, the therapeutic method was similar: First locate and identify what is at the base of the tantrums that bursts out with the proper trigger, and next, come to terms with the processing of those events.

Worth knowing

Many times fits of rage derive from previous events that cause a feeling of helplessness, in front of a danger, or even in front of degradation. By its nature, anger is an important feeling — it gives us energy to function and protect ourselves when we are hurt. However, at times it might get out of control and appear in a non-beneficial way, like when minor incidents cause a strong rage reaction. These are obviously based on more severe situations that caused us to feel threatened or hurt, that were triggered by the recent events. When the processing of this impact is complete, the tantrums lessen or even stop completely.

From a therapeutic point of view, when there are acute consequences involved, such as danger of being fired or separation from one's spouse, the first order of business is to put out the fires. This means that we work on recent events first so that they become more tolerable and will not endanger the client. Then, we can work back and process events from an earlier period that are at the core of the distress or inhibition.

Post-traumatic reaction to extreme events

Greg

Twenty five years ago, Greg was a witness to a terror attack, and was not treated. He continued on, where his business led him to move to another country in which there were frequent earthquakes. Most of the earthquakes were minor and caused minor damages, but then a very serious earthquake happened in which there were a lot of casualties and damage. He subsequently experienced panic attacks during and after each earthquake that came after. During a visit to Israel, with only two weeks left to his visit, he came to see me for several hours each day.

After one two-hour session, the terror attack was no longer affecting Greg as a traumatic memory. We started there since an acute event such as a terror attack can cause a "capsule" of hard emotions or helplessness that might come up in later cases connected to helplessness, and intensify the feeling of distress. In our later sessions, we worked on experiences from the earthquake — first on the major earthquake, and then on a series of earthquakes that increased his distress. Among them was a memory of driving across a bridge while there was a little earthquake and envisioning the bridge collapsing and him falling to his death... and his biggest fear of riding a subway after an earthquake.

Later on, we focused on "triggers" in the present, such as minor earthquakes. We finished working on the future, on scenarios involving earthquakes when Greg was in bed, in the shower, on the subway, etc. We finished only after we made sure that these scenarios in his imagination did not cause distress and he felt strong enough to face the fears. After two weeks, he went back to his business overseas; a few months later he let me know how he was doing. Greg is now able to deal with minor earthquakes, and they no longer prevent him from getting his work done. He is no longer a prisoner to his past.

Worth knowing

Even in cases of objective difficulty that cannot be changed (earthquakes, for example, or living in areas exposed to missile attacks, etc.); we can increase the feeling of resiliency through EMDR. The scenario of living our lives without any interruption or problem is unrealistic. Our happiness is dependent on our ability to face those events and not necessarily on the ability to get rid of them.

When referencing a recurring traumatic event, such as earthquakes or missile attacks, working on past events creates resilience for future events. Working on future scenarios is done by a protocol that is aimed at creating resources to face the problems, alongside building a plan for the future.

When the therapy is not working

Some of the cases in which EMDR therapy takes longer to show results, were found to be difficult cases of dissociation problems — an acute reaction to a chain of traumatic events, such as continuing sexual exploitation at various ages. (Dissociation is a condition in which a disconnection or separation is created between the person's experiences or behaviors, and the other parts of the conscious mind (thoughts, feelings, memories, actions, sense of self-identity). Dissociation can occur in varying degrees of severity). Since in dissociation there are parts of the personality that split off from each other, the regular EMDR work might influence only a specific part. In such cases, regular EMDR that was not adapted for treating dissociation might make the situation worse and there is need for integrative work. This book cannot cover the scope or depth of these cases, but I would be more than happy to refer those interested to relevant information. There are studies and books written about combining EMDR in therapy related to such serious conditions.

EMDR can also be less effective when the problem stems from a biochemical imbalance, such as depression or anxiety related to a thyroid issue, vitamin B12 deficiency, side effects of drugs, etc.

In addition, there are cases of clients who expect immediate results after just one session, and quit and leave therapy if not experiencing happier emotions. EMDR is extremely fast, yet usually not one session therapy. The interesting part is that skepticism in itself is not an issue, since it is not based on a placebo effect. As long as you work properly, even the skeptical clients will feel an improvement. In my experience with such clients, they tend to be pleasantly surprised. I personally devised a "skeptical client" form, in which the client writes the indices (indexes) in his own handwriting, before and after we start processing, so that we can compare and allow him to see the improvement for himself. In my experience, no skeptical client has used the form after the first few sessions since he sees his condition improving, and finds therapy useful.

At times, EMDR can appear to be a simple method, but, in fact, has complexities in both building the right therapeutic program (using EMDR as psychotherapy and not as a technique) and in making sure reprocessing is continuing until all channels have been cleared. In certain cases, clients do not cooperate with instructions on how to process in the room, thereby at times slowing down and perhaps even stopping the process. In such cases, it is natural for the therapy not to work in its most effective way, and the client might feel that therapy is not for him. While not complying with instructions was not part of the EMDR process, these cases can easily be fixed. At the end of the session, if the client does not feel any better, we can analyze the situation and see where the problem lies.

Hank

When Hank asked me if EMDR therapy can aid a case of stuttering, I answered that it was definitely worth a try. Since some forms of stuttering stem from emotional reasons, and even stuttering that does not stem from emotional reasons is worsened by such, alleviating the stress might help. We located the "possible suspect" memory that initiated the stuttering, and the terms of the stress that it entailed. Before processing, I instructed Hank to let the events play out in his head on their own without filtering or aiming, since during the process, it is as if you let go of the wheel and get in the back seat of the car, while your mind is driving. During processing, all you need to do is just notice what is going on during the time that you let your brain do its own thing, wherever your brain takes you is fine, just go with it. Let what is happening happen, without directing. Unfortunately Hank ignored my instructions. Every time he remembered incidents that occurred at a later age, he brought himself back to the initial incidents and tried to focus on it with all his might. As a result, the process slowed and even came to a halt.

Worth knowing

There is no problem with a situation in which free associations focus on a specific memory. However, in a situation in which associations are filtered forcefully, the process is compromised. A big part of processing might be formed by connecting the memory to later events, allowing the client to expand his point of view, experiencing events from childhood as the adult he is today. Therefore, when working on a memory and its associations, if it takes your thoughts to later events — it is very important to allow this, unless instructed explicitly otherwise by the therapist. The assumption that events occurring later are not relevant to the work associated with a specific memory is a wrong assumption. The association of memories is a process by which the disconnected memory connects to the adaptive memories network.

EMDR is not uniform. EMDR is not as simple as it might look. The risk of EMDR not working is much higher when the therapist uses it as a technique rather than applying it as psychotherapy. Do not just settle for going to a therapist with some EMDR training, but make sure you know how much and what kind of training he has undertaken (Criteria that could help in choosing an EMDR therapist can be found in Appendix D).

Besides the above-mentioned cases of dissociation, or symptoms resulting from chemical imbalance or organic reasons, most clients start feeling improvement within a few sessions after the onset of therapy, and the improvement increases as they reprocess a growing number of past events that negatively impacted them.

"It all started with a marital crisis, when I found out my wife of 12 years had been cheating on me, and felt my entire world shaken to the core. Until then, I always thought I was strong and stable and in no need of professional counseling, but the shock and instability led me to believe that even I, strong as I may be, need help. It was one of the wisest decisions I ever made.

A little personal background — I am forty years old with 2 children, a hi-tech employee with an academic background. Until the crisis, my life was very predictable, following the typical Israeli script: high school, army service, officer, South America, university, girlfriend, marriage, going abroad to study, first child, work, second child, buying a home, and a good profitable job. Everything was perfect, and then came the crisis that woke me from coma to life.

The therapy started during the marital crisis. At first we dealt with the unfolding crisis in the present. Soon enough, thanks to the associations brought up by the two "vibration tools" as I call them (they are actually two little devices you hold which vibrate alternately), it was clear to me that besides the current crisis, there were other things in the near and distant past that I needed to *understand, process, and make sure not to allow to interfere with my life in the future.*

Immediately after the divorce, I felt a big burden lifted. The burden was the path I imposed upon myself, in which I allowed myself to suffer quietly, in a bad relationship with a bitter woman whom I was always trying to please, while giving up on myself. It was very important for me to understand how I got to this point, and why. I knew I was a good, strong person, that had a lot to be proud of, but the facts were that I didn't live this way — not with my wife, nor with the environment (work, friends). This is how we started the journey I refer to as EMDR 360.

At first, the treatment felt a bit odd. We didn't sit and talk, digging into my past and soul. Instead, it kind of felt like a science experiment. I bring up a traumatic event. To a degree, I define the negative feeling it makes me feel. I hold the vibration devices, close my eyes, and associations start resurfacing, images from other events; some were very old, as far back as kindergarten. It felt odd at first, and felt unclear as to how things fit together, but the image eventually cleared up. Many things had to do with a strong feeling I've had for many years of 'not being good enough.' Regardless of the success, the degrees, the diplomas, the certificates of merit in the army and in the university, the success at work, being a great father, more often than not, the times I 'failed,' even if they were minor, made me feel as if I'm actually not good enough.

This realization was a breakthrough. I thought, 'Here, I can see what is bothering me. I might not have to continue with the therapy.' But soon enough it became clear that awareness of the problem was not enough. I had to confront these things one by one, to extinguish the coals that were still burning, and make them stop pressuring my subconscious, so that they no longer disturb my future functioning. How did it become clear? Life showed me. For example, my initial sexual performances were not as good as I expected them to be — in other words, it didn't always come up. I didn't understand how this could be, I didn't have any problems when I was married, and even after the divorce sometimes it was OK and sometimes it was not. The feeling that I was not good enough went straight to bed when new partners, especially the more meaningful ones, entered. As I've come to learn, when the subconscious presses, the body reacts.

So we identified the 'root' of the problem, and its branches where the 'not good enough' feeling disturbed the romantic, professional and family areas. In each session we cleared another obstacle along the branches from the past. We started with seemingly trivial childhood events, but they turned out to be very important because they formed the basis of my behavioral pattern. For example, in one of the sessions, the image of the kindergarten teacher whom I loved and who died of cancer that year, resurfaced. After the session, while driving, the image suddenly came back, and I burst into tears.

It turns out I had never mourned her, and felt guilty for not doing that all these years. This encouraged the feeling that I was not acting right and not worthy, and it affected other future events. Treating this event extinguished many 'burning coals,' and, in effect, freed me from the negative feelings I had about myself.

So we continued from treatment to treatment, at increasing speed, turning off the 'coals' that disturbed me all these years, that made me feel guilty and feel like I was not making the best of myself. That made me compromise with my ex-wife, all because I 'was not good enough,' and deserved to suffer in silence. We treated the intimate, personal and professional aspects, and really did a 360 degree treatment.

It is hard for me to describe the enormous impact this treatment has had on my life, on how I conduct myself in my professional life, where I am just beginning to flourish, and also in my personal life — in my relationships, in how I bring up my kids, and in my friendships as well.

More importantly, I feel infinitely stronger than ever before, ready to deal with any hardship and uncertainty without fear, because I now know that I will not conduct myself based on my past and my lack of self-worth, but instead, based on current insights into my abilities to deal with events in the here and now.

This is without question the greatest gift I could ever have given myself, and certainly due to the devoted treatment I received".

CHAPTER 4

MOVING FORWARD — EMDR FOR IMPROVING ACHIEVEMENTS

Removing internal psychological obstacles

Many experiences continue to affect us in ways that we are unaware of. EMDR therapy allows a client to become aware. From an internal understanding (as opposed to commentary by the therapist), the client sees how these events affect him in a way that holds him back, and besides awareness, the reprocessing in EMDR allows him to get rid of it.

Bill

Bill came to me to treat performance anxiety, but mentioned that his anxiety contained a component of fear of strangers (i.e., he was afraid of standing out around strangers, even if they were just a few). He told me of a turning point in his life when he was in the 5th grade. At the school graduation ceremony he got on the stage and could not speak. He remembered this as a horrible experience and had tried not to speak in front of a crowd since. I instructed him to recall the memory and follow, not direct, the associations that arose, just notice. At first, Bill saw himself read the text successfully and felt his level of anxiety decrease, but not disappear; something was still bothering him. With the next bilateral set he saw himself not only reading a text but performing an impressive dance step in front of all who were present there. The levels of distress continued to decrease, although he reported a feeling of distress still accompanying this memory. Only after the processing continued could he see himself stand on stage, paralyzed, with the "correction" being the sight of him forgiving himself for it. At that point, the feeling of distress which accompanied the memory disappeared.

After working on Bill's previous experience, he reported that he felt a decreased level of anxiety, yet still retained some fear of public speaking. While trying to understand what was stopping him, we found a memory from age five in which his tonsils were removed. This memory contributed to the belief he had of strangers hurting him. When we delved into that experience, a feeling of anger towards his parents surfaced. He felt that he was not important to them as they had not been there for him during the procedure.

The associations reached after that breakthrough, made him realize that by rebellion and resistance he had spent the next 40 years trying to get even with them. They wanted him to do well in school, so he deliberately failed. When they wanted him to go to officer's course in the army, he resisted. Due to their high expectations, he spent a lot of energy not being successful (according to their standards). Bill realized that out of spite towards his parents, he had unconsciously spent years making himself fail. Therefore, processing the memory not only aided him in speaking before strangers, but also changed other aspects of his life, such as a change in his field of occupation.

Sam

Sam, a quite wealthy and successful businessman, had difficulty with investments in his own business which limited his business development. We tried to understand what was holding him back and reached memories from his childhood. He had grown up in a small house in a relatively wealthy neighborhood where the rest of his friends were far better off socioeconomically. He was also expected to quit school and help support the family. Processing those memories helped him in changing his financial outlook; how one should behave, how to act for the good of his business, and how not to be motivated by fear of spending money, something that was rooted in what happened many years ago.

Dan

Dan, a man with a hi-tech job in his 40's, came to therapy with a personal problem. In an attempt to get to know him better, I asked him, among other questions, about his career and job security, and if he ever considered becoming self employed and going out on his own. He said, "Forget about it. I'm not good with money and trade".

Like any other negative belief, this one, too, was learned from a previous experience. It turned out that an experience at summer camp reinforced this belief. When he was six and at camp, each child had to bring something to trade with another child. Dan and his parents forgot, and he came to camp that day empty-handed. The only thing he could trade was his favorite head bandana; what he received in return was some black paper. He came home crying and when asked why, told his parents the story. They laughed at him and said, "It's better that you do not do business, it's not for you". What was meant as an innocent joke by his parents, created a negative assumption about his abilities. Even at age 45, after finishing a PhD in his field, the thought of professional and business development scared him. As a result of processing this memory, in addition to his day job, he started working as a freelancer.

Rick

Rick came to see me with very low self-esteem and feelings of constant failure. During one of our meetings he told me,

"Look, during our last set something totally unrelated came up". I responded that during processing we do not judge the contents that arise as relevant or not. We notice them and later their connection to the subject becomes clear. He told me that he saw a curtain closing and in the curtain there was a bike. "What could that have to do with the feeling of not being good enough?" he asked. I still could not answer, but promised that everything would reveal itself in time.

After another set of reprocessing, Rick could not believe what he had remembered. He said that when he was four years old and his younger sister was three years old, they both received toy bicycles. His sister learnt to ride hers before he did. This story became a family joke and the memory was at the core of Rick's feelings of failure. Our combined work on a series of similar events allowed him to walk around with a sense of ability and self-confidence.

Worth knowing

Quite often the negative assumptions clients have of themselves are ones that family members helped to create, even if not deliberately. I always listen more closely when a client describes a family joke, as there is usually a painful story behind it. Such incidents seem innocent, but leave a great impact due to the young age in which they occurred. Unprocessed memory trapped in the "capsule" would not necessarily have such an impact if it happened today, but has a stronger influence because it happened at such a tender age.

People usually perceive a lot of their characteristics as someone's personal character that cannot be changed. Often it has nothing to do with changing a trait, rather a negative internal assumption or belief that can be changed with processing in a short period of time.

Ned

Within a few years, Ned, 60 years old, lost a brother to illness and a sister in a car accident. Ned thought himself to be a strong man and felt he could deal with the sense of loss by himself. He came to me with difficulty talking to strangers, after despite trying various methods, he could not resolve this. Although he had recently experienced those devastating losses, on a day-to-day basis, there was only one thing that bothered him, which was something based on a childhood feeling of degradation. This was because today he had the capability to deal with the losses he experienced as an adult, but as a child he had a harder time dealing with lesser traumatic events from his childhood, thus those capsules of traumatic memories were created.

Worth knowing
The adverse effect of a minor incident at an age when we have insufficient resources to deal with it, may be greater than the

effect of such an event at a later age, when more resources are at our disposal. What affects whether the capsule will be created or not is resources at the time of the event, not today. This is how "capsules" can manifest in men and women who are very successful, yet at the same time feel ashamed/feel like failures/or are afraid of authority figures from events that took place when they were weaker or younger. I come across very successful people with very low feelings of self-worth. Without change there is a danger of reliving it, so that a beaten-up kid will become a beaten-up boss, etc.

Usually what creates emotional "capsules" is one of two things. The first is an incident that is acute and harsh, and the other is an incident for which we did not have the resources to cope, and therefore were overwhelmed. This can happen at a young age, but at times, other situations in which we were weak were due to surprise, or illness, something we woke up to, or the influence of drugs or alcohol.

Procrastination

Maya

Maya, studying for a Bachelor's degree in exact sciences, knew she needed to study. She had already seen what happened to her grades when she did not start studying and what happened when she did. Despite this fact, she could not bring herself to study when she should have.

Worth knowing

Procrastination can stem from several reasons. More than once I have come across clients who are stressed and suffering while studying for a test at the last moment. In fact, they create a connection between studying for a test and suffering. This situation creates a vicious circle that causes deterrence, which next time will also lead them to study at the last moment possible, etc. Like the similar process that occurs in people who are afraid of seeing a dentist and therefore put off seeing him until the situation becomes unbearable. Because of getting there late the dental treatment does cause pain and suffering, which once again makes them avoid future dental treatment. Working on past events that started the vicious circle that connected performing and suffering can stop it.

Fear of failure can also cause procrastination. In order to avoid a situation in which one studies for a test and gets a low mark on it, students prefer to avoid studying so that the explanation for the failure is much easier than coping or because they feel like there is no point in studying if they are going to fail. Processing the events that caused the connection between learning and fear of failure leads to changing the destructive pattern.

Isabelle

Every time Isabelle wanted to study for a test she would become incredibly tired. She would start yawning uncontrollably and almost fall asleep. She would wake up in the morning fresh as a daisy, pick up a book and... yawn until she could not take it anymore, causing her to just leave the whole thing alone. During therapy, we searched for previous experiences that might explain the difficulty. She remembered that several years ago she moved overseas and would work nights and study at days. During that time period, she was so tired yet still had to study. She remembered trying to study while trying to keep herself awake. The experience created a connection between studying and being incredibly tired. Working on the memory itself exhausted her, but at the end we managed to break the connection between studying and being tired, so that Isabelle could study for a long period of time without the symptoms of constant yawning.

Worth knowing
Our uncontrolled behavior is also many times a result of an experience whose effects are stored in our brain in a capsule in a raw form, because they were not processed in real time. With EMDR, we can identify the capsule and by processing it, change our automatic response.

Joe
Joe owned a successful business, but when he was required to concentrate at work on the business development of the company, he found himself doing other things. Every task he had

to finish on a deadline, he could only do under great stress, since he knew he had no other choice as well as no more time. As long as he was not committed to someone to finish on time, he would procrastinate, even while being aware of this pattern. Working on the subject, we reached a memory that had a meaningful impact on his present behavior.

Joe was injured while in the army, and because of it had to leave the prestigious unit he was in. He felt like a failure and that feeling accompanied him for two decades. He developed a chain of negative thoughts that only increased his procrastination, due to a concept by which the product of his work is meaningful only if obtained through hard work and only hard work would compensate his sense of failure. Since certain tasks that he finished easily were meaningless to him, he unconsciously made it difficult for himself by procrastinating and piling on tasks, so that the task would be achieved with effort on his part. During processing, Joe recognized other fields in his life in which this behavior was used, and he managed to link it to other cases in which he took on too much responsibility so that he couldn't manage it easily. After three sessions in which we dealt with reprocessing the injury from the army, his disappointment from having to leave the prestigious unit and the internal feelings that arose from it, he started to refuse taking on tasks beyond a certain threshold, thus stopping the vicious circle of overload and procrastination.

Another thing Joe found difficult, was delegating. He found it hard to use a professional even for home repairs and would do it all on his own. The memory that we found that was connected to this pattern was from the fifth grade, when he took his dog to the vet, who turned out to be a farm-animal vet and not a pet vet. As a result of the bad treatment, Joe's dog died and that event burned a capsule into his memory with the negative belief of "trust no one". After processing the memory with the vet, Joe told me that for the first time in his life he called an electrician, as well as a gardener, to come to his house.

Improving performance to attain peak achievements

Sal

Sal was a musician who performed often, and like many musicians he felt very anxious before and even during a performance. The way he handled the pressure before coming to me was like many other performers — mainly alcohol and drugs. Unfortunately, alcohol and marijuana at times increase anxiety, and may cause psychological dependence — a feeling that their effect is necessary in order to succeed.

First, we worked on previous incidents that gave him the feeling that he was not good enough. This was also the feeling that he would get just before major performances, increasing the level of anxiety and affecting the performance. Later on, we continued concentrating on future work, before the performances. This meant that Sal would imagine a performance in which he felt great and would repeat the scenario in his head, while stimulating both parts of the brain intermittently in order to enhance the feel of the experience, not only cognitively but also mentally and physically. After connecting to those feelings he would imagine the place in which he would perform, and the feeling of being connected only to the music, when no other stimuli could interrupt him (or as he would call it, "being in the zone").

As a result of the work we did together, he stopped being dependent on external means of relaxation, yet still found himself taking them, not out of need, but out of peer pressure. Processing several additional memories made him immune to their peer pressure. Before processing, memories in which he would get "faces" that made him feel like an outsider, or when someone would make fun of him, would make him break down and use the drugs. After processing, he felt proud saying no. Even if the rest of the band would dump on him, he would not let it affect him.

Worth knowing

While working on future scenarios with EMDR, the client recognizes emotion and sensation resources that will help him overcome the future task in a more successful manner. The resources can be, for example, a sense of ability, determination, diligence, or self-confidence. We go back to a memory that relates to that specific sensation. It can be your memory, someone you know, and if not available, even a memory from a book or a movie. After capturing the chosen memory, we strive for the most accessible and lively feeling of the sensation by using a short bilateral stimulus. When it is accessible and the client feels it, he is asked to replay the scenario or the task at hand, with this good emotion that accompanies it, in his head. The process takes several minutes, until the client feels he has completed the task successfully. In case there are difficulties during the processing — for instance, if the person sees himself as having failed the assignment — we work on the internal image of future failure as though it was a past memory and thereafter we complete the processing until it becomes positive again.

Steve

Steve began training for a marathon, and later on competed in the run many times. During his last training, he quit in the middle as he felt it was too hard. Since then he found himself unable to reinstate his regimen and was afraid of reliving the need to stop in the middle during the next run. We processed this memory, and simultaneously worked on future plans for running in the upcoming marathon. Afterwards, Steve told me that not only did he complete the run, but that he was one of the first to cross the finish line.

Brendon

Brendon was preparing to run a marathon after two years of not having run at all. He trained, and felt like he was not improving as much as he would have liked. Due to lack of time, we settled on solely working on an EMDR protocol that focuses on the future. Later on, he told me that his race results had improved by 28 minutes from the prior one.

Evan

Evan came to me when he was approaching the last semester of his Master's degree. He only had a few exams left to finish the degree. He had managed to get to such an advanced stage, despite an exam anxiety that he endured since high school. This last semester had been particularly hard on him, and he was afraid of the upcoming exams. He found himself avoiding studying. We did some work relating to EMDR and the future, in which Evan saw himself calmly studying on the days before the exam, calmly arriving for the exam, taking it, and leaving. That is what indeed happened.

Ben

Ben came to me after having completed a third of his Bachelor's in five years. He was smart and perceptive, but could not make himself sit and study. He would sign up for courses and finally not take the exam during the examination period. With EMDR, he saw himself in a future in which he sat down and studied until he finished. After that he managed to complete the next exam, and the process of improvement began. He completed the last two thirds of the B.A. program in two years.

Worth Knowing:

Working on the future could help develop powers to overcome the next assignment, but it is not a substitute for past work. As previously mentioned, if we do not treat the problem from the source, it sooner or later will return. Therefore, working on the future with EMDR is used right before a task, at the end of a session if there is only few minutes left and there is no time to open a new past memory, and of course after successfully finishing working on the past events and present triggers as the last part of the therapy.

One of the most prominent advantages of EMDR is that the capacity to cope stays with the client for a long time. This is because of the powers which work from within and not from without. In other words, it is not an idea or a suggestion coming from the therapist. In EMDR we are dealing with a personal and individual content for each individual. For example, if the difficulty is concentrating while studying for a university exam, we will together locate a memory of the client, not necessarily studying related, when he sat and concentrated successfully. We will find, for example, this moment from his childhood, when he sat for hours building model airplanes. The treatment helps the person connect to the feeling or sensation necessary and use it to deal with challenges in the future.

Personal growth

Guy

Despite the fact that Guy was quite successful in his work, while his brother had been hardly employed for years, Guy was living with the constant feeling that he was in his big brother's shadow. We worked on several memories, among them a childhood memory in which Guy's parents forced his big brother to go out and play with him and to agree that Guy could tag along with him and his friends, while Guy felt unwelcome.

We worked at a pace of one memory per session until Guy did not feel negative emotions when he remembered these feelings again. Guy felt enormous improvement yet still felt that there was something about his brother that bothered him. In the midst of processing one of the later memories, an association arose that Guy had not consciously remembered before. When he was 5 years old and his older brother was 7, their mother took them to see a mime show. When the actor chose a kid from the audience to get on stage to perform with, he chose Guy. Surprisingly, his mother took the actor's hand and put it in Guy's older brother's hand and his brother, not Guy, was the one to get on stage. This memory was not accessible to Guy on a daily basis, but when he recalled it he felt a strong negative emotion. It had sat at the base of the emotions that frequently stirred up the feeling that his brother was the preferred child and that he was living in his shadow.

Worth knowing

With the help of EMDR, we can rapidly recognize the effects of early negative experiences on our lives in the present and neutralize them. These experiences work inside us many times as a little criticizing voice. With the help of EMDR, we can recognize the key experiences that created the internal story that does not promote us, and change it to a more positive story. After successful therapy of completed processing, there is no need to fight that voice and "beat it", as many try to do, and there is no need for general rehearsals and practicing for eliminating it. Our energy does not need to show self-restraint towards past events. Energy that used to turn towards the efforts of "I will not let this little voice win", "I will fight this urge", "I will change this internal story again", can become available and be directed towards present and future development and progress.

It is true that one can progress by means of effort even when "one's feet are chained" — previous events that drag us down and make moving forward harder — but one can move forward more easily after those chains have been removed. EMDR can remove the chains.

CHAPTER 5

DEMONSTRATION OF EMDR ANALYSIS OF A SPECIFIC FIELD: FEAR OF PUBLIC SPEAKING

F ear of public speaking is a problem that is relevant to so many kinds of audiences. In this chapter, I will explain what fear of public speaking is, detail its possible causes, go over what can be done in terms of "first aid", and explain how it can be removed from its roots. It is important to emphasize that despite the fact that the following explanations concern fear of public speaking, they are relevant to other inhibitions that make functioning in real-time difficult.

The term fear of public speaking is used to describe various conditions such as: The fear of giving presentations when it comes to complex tasks, when it feels like the dynamics of exam anxiety or performance anxiety since one is being tested by "judges" and there is a fear to perform in the best way.

There are people whose difficulties in this field connect to their feeling of low self-worth or feeling like a loser, etc.

Some are even afraid of just standing up and saying their name and their profession. In such cases the problem is not fear of failing in getting the task done, but rather of being at the center of attention.

Other people have a fear of speaking in front of strangers but not necessarily before a large group of people. In other words, those individuals will not feel difficulty in front of a large group of people they know, but the presence of even a few people they do not know will be enough to cause them to clam up.

Other people have trouble speaking on camera, not in front of people. The situation causes great embarrassment even if they are alone in the room.

Fear of public speaking, like other fears, is usually created by events that have created the connection between a situation and unpleasant feelings. Sometimes it has to do with a certain failure, which is similar to the one that caused the fear of future events such as: one had a black out, failed, got negative feedback or was laughed at, and since then avoids similar situations just to be on the safe side.

Sometimes we can see people who have suffered or feared something that made them feel like "outsiders" at a younger age — they stuttered, they were poor, they wore funny clothes as kids, they were extremely short or tall, fat or thin, or wore glasses from a young age. This means that the past experience contributed to the connection that they make between being involved in a situation that put them at the center of attention, to the unwanted feeling that it procured, and the deterrence of the situation. In many cases, the connection between the event at the core of the fear and the fear in the present is unconscious. People are surprised to find out, during EMDR therapy, the strong effects that these events have on them while they are completely unaware of it. For example, a client who had studied at a religious school and then transferred to a secular school. In the religious school they would get up and greet the teacher as he walked in to class. On his first day at the secular school, he got up and greeted the teacher out of habit and was the only one to get up. The other kids laughed at him and ridiculed him. Since then, he had difficulty being in a situation in which he stands and the other people sit. He was aware of the difficulty but did not connect it with that distant memory, and connecting the two allowed us to reprocess the sooner to change the later.

That is how I worked, for example, with a 60-year-old religious man who had a fear of public speaking. When we "went back in time", he had a memory from the "cheder" (religious Jewish elementary school) when, at age 5, he was put on a chair and forced to speak. All the faces seemed threatening to him, so he drew a blank. In this case, processing that single memory helped the client tremendously.

With another client, the fear was connected to a fear of strangers, which started from some medical procedure he underwent at a young age that was burned into his memory as "strangers hurting me". The work on the incident made it easier for him to voice his opinion frequently.

Such experiences, whether conscious or not, lead to avoiding situations in which the client might be required to speak in front of an audience. There is a difference between avoidance that stems from a lack of tools and, "Only if I rehearse and prepare will I know that I have support and then I can go for it", and those in which the problem is not the number of rehearsals beforehand. What happens to them during times when speaking in front of an audience is similar to what happens in cases of exam anxiety — they can know the material perfectly, but when they get to the test, they remember nothing. Once the test is over, they recall it all. Others arrange their lives in such a way that even in advance they will not need to try, they simply avoid it altogether.

Sometimes people get anxious due to a wide variety of issues, and fear of public speaking is just a specific context. Maybe they notice fear of public speaking since it stops them professionally, but if they examine their lives, they see more and more places in which they reduce themselves unnecessarily. If the awareness is not enough and the effort is not sufficient, than going to therapy is definitely an option.

For musicians or other groups that perform frequently in front of audiences, people often have the misconception that rehearsing will make fear of public speaking disappear. I took part in a workshop where one of the participants was a musician who said he has fear of public speaking. Everyone burst into laughter and thought he was joking. He is a relatively well-known musician who performs often, so how was this possible? I went to talk to him during the break and told him that I knew he was not kidding since I had clients who are musicians and have fear of public speaking.

It is common in the music industry to "relieve" the anxiety with alcohol and drugs — which only increases the anxiety in the end. When the anxiety stems from an earlier event that was triggered, constant exposure does not necessarily ease the load but can actually press again and again where it hurts. In addition, when the problem is not dealt with at its root but by ongoing practicing, any change in the circumstances can repress the original capsule and the anxiety will return. If you got used to talking in front of twenty people, and you were invited to speak in front of two hundred, the anxiety can kick back in. You got used to talking in front of two hundred people and were invited to speak to one thousand, the anxiety might return. You got used to speaking in English and then you were invited to speak in a foreign language, the capsule can be pressed. This is because, until the original event is processed completely, the original capsule is still there and can be activated in real time.

What happens to our bodies in real time during anxiety?

We have two operating systems in our bodies — one for emergency and one for the routine. When we get stressed out from something that we perceive as some kind of threat, our bodies begin to switch over to the emergency system. With the emergency system, the blood and other resources leave the location from areas deemed less vital and are channeled to more vital systems, such as our limbs. Of the three deemed less vital systems that are affected, one is more related to us in connection with fear of public speaking.

The first system affected is the sexual system, since it is considered to be "just an extra" in time of danger.

The second system is the digestive system. At times of stress there can be stomachaches, diarrhea, nausea, or vomiting since the body is getting rid of the food so that is can take the blood and other resources from the digestive system to the emergency system.

The third system affected is the neo-cortex, the highest center of thinking in our brain. Thus in stressful conditions the ability to think clearly is affected. At this level, people cannot remember things they remembered a minute before, since it is temporarily being prevented from being accessible to them anymore. They feel a kind of restlessness and a desire to get out of the place they are in. This is actually a survival instinct.

The level of affecting thinking ability can be extremely high in extreme levels of anxiety. I had a client who was a high-ranking manager of several branches, and she went to do a certain psychological test for learning disabilities. The examiner asked her, "How much is seven minus four?" as a filter question. She could not answer and got up and left.

Of course, even while asleep she knew the answer, but blacked out in this situation of acute stress due to the effect of the emergency mode her body entered. No matter how well we know the material, how many rehearsals there are, it is just not available to us. We cannot recall or pull out of our sleeves the sorted information. Once the stressful situation has passed, we regain access to these materials. It often happens that we have decided that we know exactly what has to be done in the next stressful situation, and then when it happens we do something not necessarily related. We come out of it saying to ourselves "What in God's name was that?" This has to do with the physiological reactions of the body to the emergency system.

Of course there are different levels of anxiety. There are those who suffer from it greatly, and those who suffer from it on lower levels, but sometimes even a small level of discomfort for our body is enough to make us avoid the situation altogether.

For example, if we travel on a bus, get off at an observation point and go back on the bus, but we do not sit exactly where we sat before, we experience a kind of discomfort. This discomfort is due to the small part of the brain whose job is to keep scanning for risks. When it has already checked the place we sat in, and we find ourselves in a new place that we are unfamiliar with, there is discomfort. Here, it is about the discomfort while sitting in a new place on a bus. It is a supposedly safe place that we have been before, yet we still feel a small discomfort that is enough to make us want to sit exactly where we sat before. The fear of public speaking works much the same way, but more so. Even a low level of discomfort can cause people to avoid, even subconsciously, opportunities to speak in front of an audience.

Fear of public speaking is not the kind of problem that requires forced admission; it is about the level of annoyance and avoidance, and how much we feel it affecting us. I would recommend noticing that we do not need to wait to get professional assistance until the point where the client can no longer endure the situation.

In other words, do not wait to get help if you sense discomfort. Moreover, even if the situation is perceived as bearable, it is possible to seek therapy for improvement.

First aid for fear of public speaking

One of the things we can do in real-time, when we are going on stage or the presentation is about to begin and we feel anxious — for example if you sense a dry mouth (since the digestive system is shutting down) — is to create saliva or drink water. This forces the digestive system to start working again, and the digestive system signals the body that this is a regular situation, not an emergency. This is why, in old British movies, we see the characters talking as such, "My lord, they have all died. Let us drink some tea and come down". What does tea have to do with what just happened?! Well, drinking helps bring back the routine system into function and signaling the emergency system that it can subside.

What psychological treatments offered for fear of public speaking in the past and what they can offer today

In the past, there were methods that were less beneficial for fear of public speaking, such as talking about the past and provoking questions such as: what fear of public speaking means for you? What is this fear? How did you parents contribute to it? Etc. This is based on the wrong assumption that just awareness is enough for a real change.

Today, several methods are used, such as cognitive behavioral therapy that helps clients reveal the negative thoughts that led to negative emotions, and then tries to help people think otherwise. For example "It must be perfect or else it is not worth it", or "I must function well or else something horrible will happen", these kinds of notions will be exposed as the negative thoughts and will be argued with. The problem with this technique is that we try to fight the negative beliefs and not the reason for those beliefs. There is some level of success, but not as much as we would like.

In other forms of therapy where exposure therapy is conducted, people practice, practice, practice, and slowly the fear subsides. Unfortunately the fear subsides for the specific characteristics of the exposure so that when the characteristics change — like the size of the audience or the language in which they will speak — the process of exposure needs to be repeated. On the other hand there are people who practice, but what they are actually accumulating is failure experiences in regards to the practice itself — and thus new distress appears... Practicing above certain levels of anxiety can unfortunately lead to an escalation.

Another method is called biofeedback, in which the person is encouraged to gain more control over his bodily functions and direct it towards relaxation — for example, to regulate breathing. Here, too, there is a similar problem of trying to change the behavior and not the reason for it.

In comparison to all of these treatment methods, the framework of EMDR is different — the reason for our behavior is not fear and not negative thoughts. These are both symptoms — symptoms of an earlier capsule or capsules of memories of past events that are kept in raw form.

To deal with these symptoms what we do in EMDR is twofold:

First, we recognize the events that created the capsules that are triggered while speaking in front of an audience ("The teacher called me up to the blackboard and I went blank", or "The kids in the class laughed at me when I spoke and since then I have not raised my hand in class", or "The time that I clammed up in front of a big client and we lost him", etc.). Of course, we do not have to remember them in advance and there are ways that I mentioned earlier of locating the relevant memories during therapy. Second, we complete the reprocessing of those memories, thus stopping the relevant symptoms.

In EMDR we usually start seeing results within just a few sessions (which can be spread out or concentrated). When we speak of completing the processing of difficult events with EMDR, we speak according to the scientific literature of very high success rates (77-90%, depending on the number and nature of events) within several sessions, and usually when the issues are focused, within 3-12 sessions. This is true for less serious cases as well.

When we do not have enough time to go through the whole course of therapy — for example, when the client comes to me two days before an important task or performance — we can help him using the protocol of future EMDR. It is the same immediate process we use with athletes before competitions and with musicians before performances, which allows experiencing the situation in advance as a success story even before it actually started. Then the image of success is accessible to him in his head when it is needed in real time.

Still, it is like Cinderella and the pumpkin — meaning that the "magic" lasted only until midnight... If there is a basic deep anxiety that goes untreated, than future EMDR is something that can help for a few days at most until the regular anxiety returns. It is a treatment that can be done on an emergency basis if there are only several days before the performance and the anxiety is still present. A few weeks before a task is enough time to deal with the cause of distress in a more fundamental way, identifying and reprocessing the events that were "pressed" and routing out the fear of public speaking. Again, in EMDR we always want to hit the problem at its core and finish processing so that fear of public speaking will no longer be a part of our lives.

"As part of my occupation, I am a musician who performs several times a month. Here, too, I found myself (like many of my colleagues) dealing with anxiety during performances. After locating the formative events and their reprocessing, we used future EMDR so I could get premature positive reinforcements that helped me cope with the anxiety better while performing. This means that several days before a concert I would imagine the performance and plant some kind of positive resource (self-confidence, strength, endurance, etc.) into my mind. This significantly helped me during the performance. I enjoyed using this method in the context of social and sexual situations. Another thing I coped with was binging on sweets as a reaction to an 'emotional down.' Again, we searched for the incidents from which I acquired this behavior pattern and at the same time what the reasons for the 'down' were, and treated them as such, and that is how I managed to get rid of this obnoxious behavioral pattern as well. ... "

CHAPTER 6

ADDITIONAL INFORMATION ON EMDR

The battle over EMDR

In "The Instinct to Heal: curing depression, anxiety & stress without drugs & talk therapy" Dr. David Servan-Schreiber, psychiatrist and neurologist states:

"One of the most curious aspects of the history of the development of EMDR is the resistance it has encountered from academic psychiatry and psychology. In 2000, the most frequently used database for PTSD — the PILOTS' Database at Dartmouth Veteran Administration (VA) Hospital — recorded more controlled clinical

*experiments using EMDR than any other treatment for PTSD. **The results of these studies were so impressive that three "meta-analysis"— studies reviewing all the previously published studies — concluded that EMDR was at least as effective as the best existing treatments. In many instances EMDR also seemed the best tolerated and the fastest method".***

Since his book has been published, EMDR has already been recognized by the American Psychiatric Association and the World Health Organization, additional meta-analyses were published, and there are psychiatrists who practice EMDR. Yet those therapists who are used to treating clients using the methods which usually take much longer than EMDR (especially psychodynamic therapists and psychoanalysts) continue to resist it — and in some countries more than in others. This is of course a great misfortune that attests to the fear of progress and change.

Dr. Servan-Schreiber continues:

"Yet, today, EMDR continues to be described as a "controversial" approach in many American university circles (although it is less so in France, Holland, Germany, and England)… in the history of medicine, such controversy is commonplace. When major breakthroughs occur before their theoretical underpinnings can be explained, they systematically encounter violent resistance from entrenched institutions — especially when the treatment is described as "natural" and seems "too simple" ".

It is important to note that the disagreement between some professionals is not whether EMDR works or not. The answer to that question is certain — it works, according to every study that examined it, and there are many which found it effective, that is why EMDR is considered an evidence based therapy. The disagreements are about the exact mechanism in the brain leading to this unique effectiveness. The research in this field is evolving and there is a series of studies growing every day with conjectures about various mechanisms in the brain that may explain such unusual results. It is worthwhile mentioning that as of today, the specific mechanism in the brain that can explain how any one of the common types of psychotherapies works, is not fully explained. In other words, the requirement of knowledge on how a specific mechanism works in the brain is not a criterion that differentiates between different types of therapy, since the specific knowledge does not exist for any of the psychotherapy methods, simply because the brain has not yet been fully explored.

This poor state of affairs, described in a book published years ago, still reflects the current state of affairs in many countries. I would like to believe that it is impossible to see the literature or listen with an open mind to the clinical reports and remain indifferent to the amount of relief and help that can be available, in such a short time — a time span that is a fraction of what is offered in other therapeutic methods.

Unfortunately, many have gotten used to the preconception that what takes a short period of time must be a "quick fix". After thousands of hours of treating with EMDR, it is my opinion that this is THE "fix". Other methods only fix slower...

I invite not only the public, but also the therapeutic community to take an interest and learn more about EMDR. It is not a method just being developed; those who show interest in it can find countless papers and studies on it. Do not miss out on the opportunity to find out more.

My philosophy and worldview as a therapist

A therapeutic relationship between the client and the therapist is not an egalitarian one. It is not completely mutual, like friendship; rather, it has a hierarchy, is limited in both time and location, and, of course, costs money.

It does not resemble in any way any other day-to-day situations. Therefore change will not happen just because it exists, but rather from what will take place during this relationship.

I believe that people deserve many hours of attention — for free — from friends, colleagues, family members, etc. Therefore the goal of therapy, as far as I am concerned, is not one hour a week of paid attention. I do not offer an overpriced listening ear, but rather quality therapy in which you pay a fair price for the value you get.

I am opposed to the approach that views psychological treatment as an "hour of light in face of all the darkness", and I am in favor of using one hour to light up the whole week and later their whole life with no further need for professional help.

This way, if someone is suffering from a lack of attention in his life, instead of giving him a small piece of attention for a single hour a week and getting paid to do so — I help him get rid of the reason that causes suffering from this lack of attention in the first place. Is the problem with trusting other people? A lack of social skills? A feeling of low self-worth? Either way, we will treat it rapidly, so that the client can share his thoughts and emotions with his environment and gain attention, as it should be. Unfortunately, more than once, I've heard people who were not my clients refer to therapy as, "the only place in which someone really listens to me", while the support systems all around them collapse. I find this description not only unworthy but damaging for one's future comfort and prosperity.

Several months ago, returning from an event, I traveled by car with a young man who, like many others, opened up to me once he heard that I was a therapist. He told me about the destructive and abusive relationship he was in with his girlfriend, who caused him incredible suffering, and yet could not bring himself to get out of this situation. When I asked him what his background was, he told me that as a child his parents would beat him, especially his mother. I then asked him, if that is the case, why doesn't he seek psychological help?

Surprised at my question, he told me he had been in therapy for a year and a half and still felt no improvement. He continued telling me that even though at every session he told the therapist what happened during the previous week, he still could not understand how it can help him improve his condition. He asked me what I would do, and I replied, "I would work with you on finishing the processing of your experiences as a battered child. It seems very likely to me that there is a strong connection between the abuse you endured and your inability to break away from an abusive element in the present. When we complete the processing of your past experiences, we can see how that affects your present feelings". One week later we began working together, he grew stronger, and after a short time he was able to end the abusive relationship he was in with his girlfriend.

This case reminded me of an incident that occurred several years ago. A man approached me and told me about how he had been in a terrific therapy for the past three years, how he enjoyed going to it, and how the therapist knew him so well — "an absolute delight" he proclaimed. "Great, I am happy to hear that. What was the reason for which you originally went into therapy?" I replied. "Anxieties and an inability to form intimate relationships". He answered. "Oh, I see. And how have these issues developed since you began therapy?" His face squinted and short time after he started to see me as his therapist. After working with him and applying EMDR, the anxieties stopped. For the first time in his life he entered into a romantic relationship that lasts in fact until today.

It is because of events such as these and others, that I wrote appendix B on common myths about therapy which might cost the clients dearly. My encounters with many clients have caused me to come across many saddening examples of situations that originated from traditional assumptions of therapy.

I will never forget how one day a new client came to me, and as she walked in she looked around and asked, "Are the chairs the same height?" I answered that I had bought a pair of identical chairs, and asked why she was surprised by it. I already began to conjecture about whether she had some kind of compulsive awareness of symmetry, a common symptom of high-level anxiety. She answered me that it was because her previous therapist told her that the therapist's chair needs to be higher than that of the client. I explained to her that our roles in this room have nothing to do with the height of our seats.

Another client told how he once asked for a cup of coffee if possible, after arriving tired at his former therapist. For 50 minutes (and a lot of money) the therapist talked about what it meant that he had asked for the cup of coffee, why he had not asked for one in the past, and what it says about their relationship in the therapy room, etc. He told me that afterwards he was afraid to ask the therapist for anything, even a glass of water.

Another client told me about how dynamic therapy made her feel less intelligent than she really was — since every time she was either a little early, a little late, or right on time, it could all be inspired an ordeal of interpretation from the therapist.

I once talked to a business person who told me that the traditional therapy sounds to him like the perfect continuity program — you can always talk about what happened last week and what is happening in the therapeutic hour, as there will always be another week and another hour...

Freud was a genius in his field and a great theorist, but his writings about clients are not a research. They're mostly a collection of clients' case stories — whom he actually unfortunately did **not** help much as a therapist.

Based on thousands of hours of EMDR treatment, talking with local and international colleagues, reading hundreds of papers and following closely what is being done in the field on this type of work, I believe that EMDR brings with it great hope for mankind, and that this is the revolution we have been waiting for in the world of modern psychotherapy. I believe that every person is entitled to therapy that will help him — not slowly but greatly and in a timely fashion.

I am in favor of living up to human potential and not in its reduced form. Living in reduced psychological form when another way is possible is a saddening state of affairs, and this book is my way of contributing to this upcoming and ever-growing change. One of the reasons I wrote this book is to demystify some aspects of psychotherapy, such as the misguided perception that all that is needed is for someone to listen to you and empathically comment on the issue, and to help change current therapy in such a way that the client can connect to the powers he already possesses to complete the processing of those past events which went unprocessed in real time.

Inspired by EMDR inventor Dr. Francine Shapiro: How awareness advances scientific achievement

Dr. Francine Shapiro was a doctoral student of English literature when she was diagnosed with cancer. After she was cured, she decided to change careers, earning another doctorate — in psychology. The area she was most interested in was the mind-body connection, and how emotional distress affects physical endurance.

Many inventions in science were at first found at random, and then expanded because of the commitment by scientists to repeat the experiment time and time again. Such is the case with EMDR. Dr. Shapiro discovered one day that when she mimicked the movements that the eyes make during dream sleep (REM), it improved her mood considerably.

Most people, when first encountering a different and new situation, write it off as a strange occurrence and disregard it. Scientists, however, sink their teeth into it and "do not let go". When Dr. Shapiro noticed that something different had happened this time, she recreated what happened and how it was different from the past. She recreated it for herself and when she saw that it worked, she began doing it for all her colleagues and friends and anyone who would volunteer to try it. Then to test it, she began working with shell shocked clients from the Vietnam War. That was the basis of her doctoral thesis. By way of trial and error she went on to build a method that would originally meant to fit not only those who had undergone a negative or one-time incident, but also those who had undergone a negative emotion and suffered from post trauma and multiple traumas.

I believe that Dr. Shapiro should win a Nobel Prize for the revolution of EMDR in the psychology and health field and the contribution EMDR has had on improving millions of lives around the world. In the meantime, she has won the following awards:

- The most prestigious award for psychotherapists, the International Sigmund Freud Award for Psychotherapy of the City of Vienna, Austria.
- The American Psychologists Association Award for the trauma treatment section for outstanding advancements in the field of trauma psychology.
- The California Psychologists Association Award for Outstanding Scientific Achievements in Psychology.

ABOUT THE AUTHOR

Tal Croitoru has a B.A. in Education, Masters in clinical Social Work, Masters in Business Administration, and is a PHD student for Social Work.

In the last few years, she has been working as a psychotherapist and certified EMDR consultant in her private practice, manages a national chain of EMDR clinics, and has been lecturing since 2007 at the University of Haifa, Department of Social Work.

Since realizing the potential of EMDR to change millions of lives in a relatively short time, she has devoted her life to internationally expanding the reach of EMDR by lectures, informational products, a professional EMDR network, and books.

You can find more about her work and get access to EMDR resources on her sites:

www.TalCroitoru.com
www.TheEMDRRevolution.com
www.emdrexperts.com
She can be reached at tal@emdrexperts.com

ACKNOWLEDGMENTS

First of all, I would like to thank Dr. Francine Shapiro. Thanks to her curiosity and courage the lives of millions worldwide have changed by now, including the lives of myself and my clients. Very few people could do what she did. The world looks a better place thanks to people like her.

Without Dr. David Servan-Schreiber who wrote the book "The Instinct to Heal", I would never have heard about EMDR. His death is a huge loss, and I'm glad I was able to thank him while he was still alive.-

EMDR Israel is an NGO that trains EMDR therapists and consultants in my home country of Israel. I owe a lot to it and its leadership for helping me start my journey in EMDR. This NGO makes Israel one of the most productive countries in terms of using and developing new EMDR protocols.

I would like to thank EMDRIA — EMDR International Association, and its active discussion list of thousands of EMDR therapists around the world, that help us all to constantly learn from each other, and HAP — the international Humanitarian EMDR projects NGO (www.emdrhap.org) that constantly reminds us all how much EMDR can help even in the most difficult situations.

I am grateful to my clients and my employed therapists who enabled me to take part in changing the lives of so many people. I am grateful for each and every one of you.

And finally I would like to thank my supportive family and friends, for the patience and support shown in day to day life and while writing this book. Behind any creative person there is a group of people who support and enable the creative process to occur; I am lucky to have behind me such supportive people: Oren Ben Ami, David and Hanna Croitoru, Jacob Lubinsky, Ofer Beith Halachmi, Orly Traubichi, and Gili and Lior Kama.

WHEN SHOULD ONE GO TO THERAPY AND HOW CAN IT HELP?

In short: One should go to therapy when experiencing emotional pain and suffering, or internal obstacles that get in one's way.

More comprehensively:

A. When suffering from: anxiety, nightmares, tantrums, crying attacks, inferiority complex, depression and desperation, as well as compensating behaviors like food, sex or shopping, etc.

From time to time, we can all experience these feelings, however, when suffering from indications of more severe distress such as the intensity of the feeling, the frequency in which you experience it, as well as its implications in other areas of your life, one should consider getting help.

B. When dealing with a crisis or struggling with difficulties experienced in the past, or coming up in the future such as: attacks, car accidents, loss of a close friend or loved one, as well as more common experiences like separation, rejection (socially or romantically), failure and termination, or layoffs at work.

C. When experiencing feelings of paralysis in life, feeling as if you are stuck in a 'dead end' without the ability to move forward or change it. This includes difficulties with interpersonal relationships, with career aspirations or advancements, as well as a general feeling of emptiness and lack of life goals.

Examples:

*   Struggling with traumatic events — accidents, attacks, terror event, death of a close friend or loved one, etc.
*   Struggling with a life crisis — betrayal, separation, divorce, job termination, unemployment, postpartum depression, etc.
*   Coping with anxiety and phobias — fear of public situations, exam anxiety, performance anxiety, fear of dogs, dental phobias, recurrent nightmares, etc.

- Changing repetitive behavior patterns — difficulties with intimate relationships, tantrums, repeated bad decision making, indecisiveness, procrastination, etc.
- Eliminating internal obstacles to achieve your personal best — for athletes looking to boost their performance results before a competition; for students before important tests, SAT's or psychometric exams, etc.; for artists before performances and auditions; and at work for business people looking to improve their ability to mount successful presentations and negotiations, and improve their self-worth before a request for a raise or promotion.

Test yourself:

- Do you experience negative feelings for a significant length of time, or as the result of a crisis or event, that do not seem to improve on their own?
- Do you feel that you have internal obstacles that prevent or inhibit you from advancing and breaking through, even though in theory, you know what needs to be done?
- Have you noticed that you exhibit patterns of behavior that hinder you in your personal or professional life, that awareness alone does not prevent you from repeating?
- Do you have unpleasant feelings, or fears and concerns that prevent you from speaking before an audience, cause you to feel uncomfortable being the center of attention,

and block you from advancement in your personal or professional life?

- Do you have a challenging sports-related, professional or personal task awaiting you, and you need specific reinforcement to give you the boost you need to accomplish it?

If you answered YES to even one of the above, relevant treatment can help.

How can therapy help?

- **Aiding in understanding ourselves and our environment** — many different types of treatment are built on the assumption that when a person is aware of what drives him, his problems will be solved. As a result, treatment focuses only on producing **awareness** of the internal emotional processes. In fact, this is very inadequate, as there needs to be another stage beyond awareness and will — the **ability** to change.
- **Obtaining new tools** — to gain insight and revelation, for coping and emotional processing, and for encouragement in trying out new experiences.
- **Reprocessing of memories and negative events from our past** — completing the processing of experiences that continue to negatively affect us and prevent us from moving forward.

SEVEN COMMON (AND COSTLY) MYTHS ABOUT PSYCHOTHERAPY:

A. Thinking that as long as there is a good reason to be depressed / stuck, nothing can help.

First, there are several measurements of emotion. One of them is the general direction of the emotion — positive or negative. This is a dominant measurement but is not the only one, and settling for it helps distress thrive without turning on the warning signals. Additional criteria should be pointed out to recognize distress and consider the need for help:

1. The intensity of the emotion.
2. Its prevalence — how frequent is it?
3. Ramifications — how much does it influence and decrease function?

Ignoring these criteria legitimizes the decline, because "the person has a good reason to feel bad" and might miss signs indicating the need to turn for help. Secondly, a difficulty does not have to be completely detached from reality for there to be a way to treat it properly. It is possible to work on building up your strength in light of a difficult reality or even chronic conditions.

I'll give an example, EMDR therapy serves to treat those affected by an earthquake. Some people wonder, "What's the point? It's not nice to say, but there will be another one soon". The answer is that if we do not process the earlier memories of earthquakes properly, every subsequent earthquake triggers the previous ones and thus increasing our anxiety level. In contrast, when we do process the earlier memories properly, not only does the earthquake not trigger the anxiety of previous earthquakes, but we have an accessible feeling of resiliency and survival from the previous events. Thus reprocessing of past events builds within us a resiliency toward future events.

B. Thinking that the maximum we can hope to gain with treatment is awareness, and awareness combined with self discipline is enough to create change.

Many types of therapy are built on the notion that the minute someone acknowledges what is bothering him and knows its origins this alone will solve most of his problems. Respectively, the treatment focuses on creating an awareness of the processes that form him interpersonally and psychologically. In actuality, for a change to take place one not only needs awareness, but also the ability to bring about that change. It is really not enough to acknowledge the specific behavior pattern or its origins. Many times, there is a need for a deep psychological shift and not just awareness, in order to bring about the change in behavior.

Furthermore, with the right treatment, we can achieve much more than just a slow awareness of a pattern of behavior; we can achieve a significant change to that pattern within a few short weeks. At times, self-discipline can help, but most times it is far from enough. We can achieve results in an effective way with reprocessing the roots for those patterns. Then the energy we used in order to overcome the experiences and obstacles from the past is no longer needed there and can be allocated in other fields — for our personal growth and development.

C. The thought that there is a standard or uniform treatment method.

This approach leads many people to feel that treatment will not help them because of past unsuccessful or ineffective stabs at it. Sometimes they even blame themselves and say upsetting things like, "I am obviously screwed up and cannot be fixed". This is a serious mistake. Irrelevant treatment might not help and can sometimes harm, but a relevant therapist in relevant treatment can be very helpful within a very short window of time.

Research and experience shows that even people who did not make progress with many years of psychotherapy using one method can be assisted by other treatment methods within a few weeks or months.

D. Confusing depth with length when it comes to therapy.

In actuality, therapy can also be long and superficial, or short and substantial. The substance of the treatment is not a matter of time, but about what is brought up in treatment, as well as the level of change that is created. In other words, to what extent is it a fundamental shift and not just cosmetic? EMDR is sometimes referred to as "psychoanalysis on speed" not only because it touches upon the issues in depth, but also because of the speed and short length of time in which it allows you to process the memories and find insights and relief.

Sometimes people tend to look negatively at it, calling it "quick fix therapy". I propose to think about the point of reference when it comes to length. It is possible to look at the quick therapy in exactly the opposite light — as an effective means for significant results — and consider slower therapies as an unnecessary lengthening of therapy.

E. Considering the cost of a single session and not the cost of the entire therapy (cost per session multiplied by the number of sessions).

First of all, I need to state, that in my opinion, therapy that does not yield results, even if given for free, is still costly; however, in this context I will be referring only to the monetary aspect. You need to do the math to know how much therapy really costs you. Therapy that takes two or even three years is not unusual .Multiply the cost of a session in 100-150 weeks, and this is the actual monetary cost of therapy. Even one year of therapy, which is considered fairly short, with those same conditions is the cost per session times 50 weeks.

In contrast, with the quicker, more effective therapy, one that usually does not stretch beyond a few weeks for focused reasons or a few months for more complex ones, even if the therapist charges somewhat or even a lot more per session, the therapy itself still costs you much less in comparison to the previous option.

F. To compare the total cost of therapy to zero, rather than the cost of not getting therapy at all.

Suffering, feeling stuck, and internal obstacles affect us not only psychologically but also financially. Fears, anxieties, low self-esteem, and crises that are reflected in the professional arena, and cause us to underperform at work might lead to:

For salaried employees:

- Increased odds of termination (being laid off), lessening your chance of promotion (because your work is not noticeable, or you do not feel confident asking for the promotion)
- Decreasing your chance of finding new work
- Avoiding requests for a raise

For the self-employed:

- Missed opportunities to advance and gain clients/ be at the forefront
- Procrastination (so that profitable projects are postponed)

Suffering, fears, anxiety, low self-esteem, and crises that manifest in the personal arena can all cause financial stress alongside the emotional one.

Difficulties with intimate relationships cause not only heartbreak but also prevent us from having a life partner to share living costs and raise children with. For example, the financial cost of divorce is much higher than the cost of spending time working on the relationship; the financial cost of a nasty divorce is much higher than the cost of therapy to work out friendly one; and, of course, as long as we are feeling better there is less of a need for expensive behaviors (I'll go to X, buy Y, and then I'll feel better for a while) to compensate for feeling bad.

G. Disconnecting goals — the confusion between the means and the purpose, where the relationship with the therapist becomes the end and not the means, at the expense of the purpose of the therapy.

Of course, it is important to have a good foundation in the relationship to the therapist, so that the therapy will show results. Secondly, a good therapeutic relationship can be an anchor and provide encouragement and support that lend a hand during difficult times, as well as a source of strength to overcome other life challenges. Thirdly, we can learn about ourselves and our relationship from the interaction that takes place in the therapeutic relationship itself, examine, see and practice what we can do otherwise, and implement this understanding outside the treatment room.

However, confusion between the means and the end (or purpose) can develop. People who are in therapy for a long time, years actually, come and tell me that they had an amazing connection with another therapist who understood them and made therapy enjoyable, however, when we actually look into the reason they went to therapy to begin with and how much their situation has improved, we see very little movement or sometimes none at all.

Therapy is a means and not the end (or purpose) and so too is quality therapy. In order to prevent the confusion I just described, it is important to know the reasons why we are looking into therapy to begin with, or what are the reasons for continuing treatment, and regularly check in to see if there are any improvements or advancements in our lives in and out of the therapy session.

CRITERIA FOR CHOOSING PSYCHOLOGICAL TREATMENT

You are not content with your current reality. You want a change, but there are so many options, so many methods and techniques. How can you tell which treatment method to choose? The four problems people encounter when choosing psychotherapy are:

1. **Reliability** — how can I know the treatment method is reliable as opposed to useless "ruminations", the types that cause so many people to lose faith in psychotherapy to begin with?

2. **Effectiveness** — how can I know the treatment method will help as soon as it can and not prolong my suffering as well as incur additional costs?

3. **Professionalism** — how can I tell the person treating me is the best person to treat me and not a charlatan; and that I am in good hands?

4. **Results** — how can I know as soon as I can that the treatment is really working and I am not just wasting time, money and effort?

The solution to these problems should be in choosing a proven, reliable, professional, effective therapy, and not less importantly — a fast and measurable one.

I wrote down the relevant criteria I suggest using in choosing the right therapy method, and in brackets I answered those questions regarding EMDR.

Reliable

1. Is this a scientifically proven method with dozens of studies proving its effectiveness? (YES (1))

2. Are there internationally recognized treatment organizations who verify the effectiveness of said method? (YES (2))

Effective

3. Are there studies that have compared this method to other treatment options and found it preferable? (YES (3))

4. Can you feel a marked improvement after only a few sessions; and with more specific target goals, the overall therapy is only a few sessions long? (YES)

Professional

5. Are those authorized to use this therapy professional therapists, and have they received sufficient training? (You need to check personally — see next appendix for details.)

6. Do the therapists receive regular training and consultations in order to be on the cutting edge of clinical and theoretical knowhow? (You need to check personally — see next appendix for details.)

7. Are the therapists also experienced with complex cases so that they can address difficult situations when necessary? (You need to check personally — see next appendix for details.)

Measurement

8. Is there a way to know if treatment is working? Are there measures that measure improvement within the session

itself, as well as out in the real world, at regular intervals? (YES).

How is help given

9. Does it provide tools? Does it help you deal with confrontation? Does it figure out what the issues are? Does it get rid of the root of the problem? (Awareness is not enough to allow change. Tools can greatly assist us, but only up to a point. EMDR treatment gets rid of the source of the problem, to the extent that one no longer needs the treatment.).

10. Is it necessary to do 'homework' or assignments outside of the therapy sessions? (NO)

(1) A long list of studies verifies the effectiveness of EMDR. See a short list in the following link: http://www.emdrhap.org/emdr_info/researchandresources.php#trials

(2) Including: The American Psychological Association, The American Psychiatric Association, and the U.S. Department of Veteran Affairs (for treatment of Vietnam veterans), the British Ministry of Health and more. See a list of leading therapeutic bodies that recognize the effectiveness of EMDR in the following link: http://www.emdrhap.org/emdr_info/researchandresources.php#treatment

(3) See a list of sample studies, including studies comparing EMDR to other treatment methods that found that EMDR helped within fewer sessions, in higher rates and with fewer dropouts.
http://www.emdrhap.org/emdr_info/
researchandresources.php#trials

RECOMMENDED CRITERIA FOR SELECTING AN EMDR THERAPIST

EMDR is a method that requires skill. To think that its essence is only "bilateral stimulus" or "eye movement" is like saying that the basis of traditional therapy is lip motion.

A client once told me that after a TV show he had seen several years ago by psychiatrist Dr. David Servan-Schreiber, he tried to help his girlfriend, who had been through trauma, at home. The result was that her distress worsened and she even tried to kill herself. It is a powerful method, and there is an excellent reason that EMDR can be done only by certified mental health therapists to begin with.

The difference between EMDR therapies with an experienced therapist vs. a non-experienced therapist can be as big as the difference between heaven and earth with respect to the time frame and the timetable. I had clients who had tried EMDR therapy before that did not succeed for this reason.

Despite the fact that the protocol is very structured about specific memory, there is a need for know-how, skill and experience in building a therapeutic plan, as well as the ability to intervene during therapy if the therapy gets stuck. Since the role of the EMDR therapist is to allow processing to take place, he is the one to regulate, the one to make sure that all four channels (sensory, cognitive, emotional, somatic) are processed, and the one who knows what has gone wrong and how to assist if the distress remains.

One can treat with EMDR even after the first level of training is complete, but only after the second level can one concentrate on building a full EMDR therapeutic plan — an important element that could be the difference between a fast and successful therapy and one that is not.

Unfortunately, most therapists do not receive training beyond the primary level. My recommendation is not to see a therapist who has not completed second level or above of EMDR. The first level is far from enough.

I recommend seeing a therapist who has:

1. Been properly certified as an EMDR therapist or
2. Finished the second level of EMDR training and has regularly taken part in EMDR supervision.

Being one who has interviewed therapists in order to decide whom to hire as a therapist for the chain of clinics that I manage, I have met and spoken to hundreds of them. Unfortunately, I often encounter therapists who completed level 1, and stopped there (and at times without much practice using the method), or therapists who have stopped going to supervision sessions, so that they, in fact, rely on their real long-term memory regarding how exactly the method is applied. The connection between them and EMDR is quite often purely coincidental.

Do not give up on the following points! It can be the difference between the extremely effective results described in the book, and a therapy that is much longer and less effective. Ask your therapist:

1. How many levels of EMDR training did you complete? (Look for level 2 and above).

2. Can you and do you use EMDR as psychotherapy, not just as a technique? (Look for EMDR as psychotherapy).

3. Can you and do you use EMDR as a "stand-alone therapy"? (Look for the ability to use EMDR as a standalone therapy).

4. How many hours of EMDR do you practice a month? (Look for a 2-digit number).

5. How many supervision sessions of EMDR have you been in since finishing your basic training? (Look for at least 10 sessions of EMDR supervision in the past year).

EMDR is psychotherapy, not a technique. A therapist who regards it as a technique misses out on a big portion of the way in which you can be helped using EMDR. **A therapist who is not kept up to speed and does not keep in shape with regard to his EMDR skills is far from being able to assist you in the best way possible.**

FIRST AID IN
CASE OF EMERGENCY

What happens to us?

- Our body has various mechanisms to lead us back to perfect health — be it for a physical need such as a cut or fracture to the body that changes and repairs itself over time, or for a psychological need that our brain tries to process right away, when we're awake and also while asleep, through dreaming.

- When dealing with an overwhelming situation or occurrence, and when not at our full strength (either due to weak states such as fatigue or illness, or helplessness due to young age), our brain is flooded and unable to fully process the event in real time.

- The results are that the memory of that event is stored in the brain in a raw and not fully processed form with the thoughts, feelings, body sensations, pictures, sounds & smells of the event.

- This means that whenever an external stimulation in the present relates to the unprocessed content, it is re-experienced, in raw form. So, the same harsh emotions from the past event are re-lived, in disproportionate intensity.

- We may feel one or more of the following:
  ◊ More irritable
  ◊ Sadder / more sensitive
  ◊ Restless (mentally or physically)
  ◊ More anxious (wanting to avoid things we didn't avoid in the past)

- We might experience flashbacks — parts of the event (images, smells or sensations) will resurface involuntarily when dreaming or when awake

Some bad news, (but not to worry, there will be better news coming up):

- Memories that did not process properly are kept in a raw form in our brain, separate from properly processed memories that may have occurred earlier or later, and will not change, even after newer information.

- An example is PTSD — a slammed door can sound like a shooting gun, and takes the person back to the battlefield. Even when new experiences have been added to the general memory network, and we are fully aware that years have passed since the battle, the raw content is still there and the minute it is triggered, takes us back to that event and starts playing itself out.

- Similarly, we can feel very intense sensations of danger to us or to our loved ones, even though we know cognitively that we are safe, or that the intensity is unjustified.

Beware of myths

- **"It is enough to give information that the danger has passed and the feeling will disappear".** Knowledge and reason have no effect on the sense of danger. A person suffering from PTSD knows that the war has long passed, but the sights and signals, when triggered, continue to play out in a raw manner. This is because knowledge and reason belong to the general memory network, and the content of the war is raw and stored separately. The two parts are not accessible to one another.

- **"You just need to give it more time".** When referring to material stored in our memory in a raw fashion, it does not matter how much time has gone by. The reality is that material that does not process properly in real time, can accompany us for years, as if experienced for the first time or like it happened just yesterday.

- **"A traumatic event can shape and strengthen our character".** This is not necessarily true. Memories stored in a raw manner that can play out by a stimulus in the present, do not shape us but, rather, weaken us. Also, the psychological damage that plays out in subsequent events that remind us of the core event only grows.

Now, for the good news...

Prevention and first aid

There are things that can be done immediately after a difficult experience, to help our memory process properly, and to lessen the danger that it will be stored in a separate 'capsule'.

- Let the body know it can take its guard down and the danger has passed, by ensuring proper eating and sleeping habits, as well as proper sports and physical activity. Otherwise, the body still feels as if it is in a state of emergency. It is still tense and looking for danger and this might create a situation where there are not enough resources to allow proper processing.

- Reduce the consumption of anxiety inducing substances (nicotine, caffeine — coffee, tea, soft drinks that include caffeine like cola, alcohol, drugs).
- Do not bury the experience but rather look for sources of support.
- Ensure the correct attribution of responsibility — self-blame increases anxiety and interferes with our ability to deal with and overcome distress.

Treatment

- Science has progressed in recent years to the point that there are now innovative methods in the trauma field that no longer stop with being a listening ear, providing awareness or doling out tools, but allow us to come full circle with processing our raw memories that were not dealt with in real time, and can do so in a surprisingly short amount of time.
- You can now fully process your memories of any single trauma with the help of EMDR, a treatment method designed to help with trauma related issues within the average of up to 4 — 5 hours (for 80% of cases).
- When dealing with multiple traumas, a systematic work method is required, usually in chronological order.
- Treatment can show results within a matter of hours that can be done in sequence, or one day after another.

- After processing, the event no longer activates in a raw manner as it did in the past, even if it is a serious trauma like an attack, natural disaster, accident or eyewitness to a death or injury.
- Bereavement is a unique situation which is harder to overcome and process, yet we can still reduce the pain in a significant manner.

HOW TO KNOW IF ONE IS RECEIVING A SUCCESSFUL THERAPY?

You have decided to seek treatment, you have chosen a therapist. Some time passes, perhaps even a few months and you attend a few sessions. The question arises: How do I know if therapy is working?

I would like to offer a few criteria to weigh the situation. I will split them in two: within the therapy session, and out in the world at large.

Within the confines of the therapy session:
- Confidence in the ability of the therapist to help you.
- Does the therapist display understanding and empathy?
- Is there a sense of openness and trust?

- A sense that if there is a disagreement or even an insult, it is not malicious and can be addressed and dealt with.

Outside the confines of the therapy session:
Here the criteria change in relation to the reason for seeking treatment.

Weakening or disappearing symptoms like: fewer tantrums, nightmares, less of an inferiority complex, and less anxiety. Or, a rise in:

- Hope
- Self-esteem — a feeling of competence and personal ability
- An understanding of the self and the environment around you
- A rise in the tools we utilize to deal with and improve our day to day life
- Improvement in life functions: employment, interpersonal relationships, family relationships, finding meaning in life and more
- Positive change in our approach to the world and how we view it

If we doubt we are getting the right treatment, it is important to look to the reasons we searched out treatment to begin with and to check how the treatment is affecting them. Make sure you are not judging the therapy based on criteria that are not relevant. The common mistakes in this context are:

- The depth of connection to the therapist. As I wrote before, the relationship with the therapist is the means, not the end. Trust, comfort, and security in the treatment room are all important to successful treatment, but the ends should not shift. The central aim should be improvement outside the treatment room.

- Depth of self-awareness. The level of self understanding that the client acquires regarding the source of his suffering and problematic behavior patterns is only the first stage. Awareness is usually not enough to initiate change; the client needs to acquire the ability as well. Ability is built through two main processes:

  1. Removing the shackles — the memories of traumatic events that tend to continue haunting us and adversely affect our present behavior. The best way I know to process disturbing memories is by utilizing the EMDR therapeutic method.

  2. Providing new tools (for thinking, analysis of situations, coping and emotional processing) and encouragement to engage in new experiences.

COMMON POSITIVE AND NEGATIVE BELIEFS

Negative Beliefs	Positive Beliefs
I am not good enough	I am good enough just the way I am
I am not smart enough	I am smart enough
I am not worth anything	I am valuable
I am a loser	I am a winner
I am unloveable	I am loveable
I am hopeless, screwed up	I can improve
I am an idiot	I am intelligent
I do not count, I am insignificant	I count, I am important

There is something wrong with me	I am healthy, at peace with myself, can deal with things
I am ugly, repulsive	I am pretty, attractive, fine just the way I am
It is my fault, I am guilty	I am innocent, I can forgive myself
I should have done something else	I did the best I could
I am a bad person	I am a good person
I am embarrassed of myself	I have self-respect, I deserve respect
I deserve bad things	I deserve good things
I cannot trust my judgment	I can trust my judgment
There is something wrong with me, I am disappointing	I am fine just the way I am
I deserve to die	I deserve to live
I deserve to be miserable	I deserve to be happy
I'll never change	I can learn from the past and improve
The world is fundamentally bad	The world is fundamentally good/neutral

I am fundamentally bad	There are good and bad things within me
I have a terrible future ahead of me	I have a great future ahead of me, I can influence my future
I am in danger, I feel unsafe	It is over, I am secure and protected now
I am fragile, vulnerable, I can be crushed	I am durable, strong
I am going to die	I have survived
There is nothing to live for	I can find what to live for
I cannot take it, cannot deal with it	I can deal with it
I am not in control	I am in control, I can deal with it
I am helpless	I have a choice
I am weak	I am strong
I cannot take care of myself	I can take care of myself
I have to be perfect, satisfy everyone es' requests	I can be myself

PERSONAL MESSAGE FROM THE AUTHOR:

If you have been to an EMDR therapy, you already know how life changing it can be, in amazingly short time.

I want you to be an active part of The EMDR Revolution. Look around you — there is so much needless suffering and unused potential in our world — you can let more people know how life can be with the help of EMDR.

I'll be grateful if you choose to send your personal story of your experience with EMDR (you can omit any recognizing details if you choose to) to the book's site www.TheEMDRRevolution. com, or to my personal email: tal@emdrexperts.com.

Selected stories will be published, including in my new coming books, and will help to spread the word out.

Thanks in advance,
Tal Croitoru